KU-004-374

COMPENDIUM OF JEWELLERY MAKING TECHNIQUES

350 Tips, Techniques and Trade Secrets

XUELLA ARNOLD
& SARA WITHERS

Search Press

A QUARTO BOOK

Published in 2013 by Search Press Ltd

Wellwood

North Farm Road

Tunbridge Wells

Kent TN2 3DR

Reprinted 2014

Copyright © 2013 Quarto Inc.

All rights reserved. No part of this publication may
be reproduced, stored in a retrieval system or
transmitted in any form or by any means, electronic,
mechanical, photocopying, recording or otherwise,
without the permission of the copyright holder.

ISBN: 978-1-84448-937-4

Conceived, designed and produced by

Quarto Publishing plc

The Old Brewery

6 Blundell Street

London N7 9BH

QUAR.TTSJ

Color separation in Hong Kong by Modern Age Repro
House Ltd
Printed in China by 1010 Printing International Ltd

FOR QUARTO
Project editor Chelsea Edwards
Designer Austin Taylor
Photographer Philip Wilkins
Illustrators Kuo Kang Chen and John Woodcock
Picture researcher Sarah Bell
Copyeditor Liz Jones
Proofreader Claire Waite Brown
Indexer Helen Snaith
Art director Caroline Guest
Creative director Moira Clinch
Publisher Paul Carslake

Contents

continued →

Forewords

I have always loved designing and making objects of all types, but when I specialised in jewellery and silversmithing at college I had found my chosen medium in metal and decided to make it my career, which has kept me busy learning and creating ever since.

Jewellery is a large and fascinating subject in which you can never stop learning, whether it is a new technology, technique or material. I hope that the ideas, techniques and tips in this book will help you along the way, to whatever level you want to go, and lead you to discover what is possible within the exciting subject of jewellery making.

Xuella Arnold
(Chapters 3, 4 and 5)

I have always enjoyed the colours, shapes and diversity of beads, and have made them the main focus of my work. People have made jewellery throughout history, which is something that really appeals to me. We may now have all the advantages of sophisticated materials and tools, but we are basically doing what people have done for centuries, adorning ourselves and making a statement about ourselves with our jewellery.

The aim of this book is to give you the core skills that you need to turn your creative ideas into a reality – plus some extra insider information that comes with experience. We hope the book will take you in new directions and open you up to different jewellery processes and practices.

Sara Withers
(Chapters 1, 2 and 6)

About this book

From chapter two, 'Using wire'

Beginners start here!
If you're new to jewellery and don't know where to begin, we've flagged some entry-level techniques.

'Fix it' panels
These appear regularly and offer ways to solve problems or avoid common pitfalls.

From chapter four, 'Metalwork techniques'

Save money!
The authors point out ways to improvise tools and make your raw materials go further.

Finished projects
Beautiful finished pieces of jewellery will inspire you with ways to implement new techniques and help you create your own designs.

'Try it' panels
These pop up throughout the book and contain tips and tricks for methods you may never have thought of trying.

Pearl and silver necklace
*Learn how to fix a fastener with crimps
using tip number 21 on page 17.*

CHAPTER ONE

Threading and beading techniques

This chapter will help you hang your pendants and demonstrate how best to showcase beautiful beads. If you want to re-thread some old jewellery or learn about knotting techniques, you'll find tips here to help you achieve the look you want.

Threading tools

You can start to make necklaces and bracelets without buying a huge number of tools. Shown here are the main ones you will find useful, along with descriptions of the threads that you might choose to use.

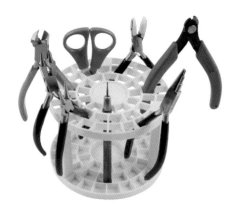

Your basic tools will be a pair of chain-nose pliers or crimping pliers, both of which are used to squeeze crimps onto threads to attach a fastener or create spaces between beads. Scissors, of course, are always useful. If you are working with beading wires, use heavy-duty scissors or old wire cutters – don't use the kind of delicate wire cutters suitable for the wirework shown on page 30, since you will blunt them.

You will need a few needles for fine, soft threads and possibly some beeswax to help with the threading. Another useful tool is a reamer, which clears the holes in beads and can be used to smooth any roughness inside them.

1 Getting set up

Think about your comfort. You don't need to be in a proper workshop; you can spread out on any table. Remember that good light is your most important tool. Think about your seating position, too – you may be here for many hours, so make yourself comfortable and remember to take regular breaks.

3 Storing your tools

A pencil case or small make-up case makes a great carrying pouch for your tools. However, if you have the luxury of a designated work table, you can store your tools on that in pots or old mugs. If you start to work with jewellery wire as well as threads, you will need a larger selection of tools. An acrylic tool rack is a great way to keep a selection of tools ready for use.

FIX IT

4 MAGNIFIER LAMP
If you have tried repositioning your lights and are still struggling to see intricate work, try using a magnifier lamp or a neck magnifier.

2 Matching tools to threads

The tools that you need will relate to the threads that you choose.

THREAD	FINISH WITH	ESSENTIAL TOOLS
Beading wire: tigertail, Beadalon, Soft Flex, illusion cord	Crimps	Chain-nose/crimping pliers + heavy-duty scissors/ old wire cutters
Soft threads: silk, polyester, linen, leather, cord, ribbon	Knots	Needles, scissors
Soft threads: silk, polyester, linen, leather	Crimps	Crimping pliers, needles, scissors
Elastic, illusion cord	Knots	Needles, scissors, glue

5 Choosing your threads

There are many choices available to you for threading a necklace or a bracelet, ranging from silk to strands of steel. Your main considerations will be the weight of your beads and the size of their holes. Always use the strongest thread that you can.

Soft threads These are made of natural materials such as silk, linen or hemp – and all of these can be finished with knots or crimps. They hang well and you can knot between beads. Thicker threads are useful if you have large holes in your beads.

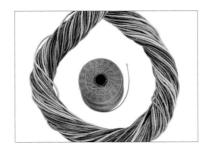

Beading elastic Modern elasticated thread, such as Stretch Magic, comes in different thicknesses and works very well for bracelets, especially if you are not sure of the size that you need to make or don't want to have a fastener.

Beading wire This is steel cable covered in nylon, such as tigertail or Beadalon. Don't confuse it with jewellery-making wire, shown on pages 30–31. The softer kinds of beading wire can be knotted, but generally work better with crimps. They are very strong for their diameter and are easy to thread. They are great for bracelets, but can look a little stiff if your beads are quite light.

Leather or cotton cords These are great for hanging pendants from – they can be finished with knots or leather crimps. Be careful with some of the finer leather cords, though, because they are not very strong.

Synthetic soft threads and illusion cord Polyester threads are available in different thicknesses – they can be used for knotting or with crimps. They are very strong and some are ready-waxed. Nymo is a good choice if you are working with tiny beads. Illusion cord or monofilament is a strong, synthetic material that is useful when you want to space your beads and create a 'floating' look.

shown on pages 30–31.

TRY IT

6 EXPERIMENTING WITH THREAD
Remember that not all threads have to come from bead shops. Try exploring your local haberdashery or knitting shop for yarns and ribbons. You could even look up boat-making suppliers – there are some excellent threads available that are intended for making and mending sails.

7 TROUBLE THREADING
If you are having trouble with the odd bead that does not want to thread, try using a reamer or round file to clear the hole in your bead. You can also make yourself a substitute needle by folding a piece of beading wire to help pull the thread through.

FIX IT

TRY IT

8 INTEGRAL NEEDLE
If you are looking for a fine thread that you can use in knotted work without the extra thickness of a separate needle, you can buy packets of silk thread with an integral needle. Remember to unwind the length of the thread and knot the plain end, so that you get full use of the needle.

Design principles

For some jewellers, developing design ideas is the hardest part of the process. Others are brimming with ideas but have trouble working out how to construct them. The pages that follow will help you out, whichever approach you need to take.

Multi-strand dichroic glass necklace
Pieces of dichroic glass wired with closed loops and threaded onto beading wires.

9 Record your inspiration

Keep a sketchbook or notebook with you at all times, or store ideas on your phone (remember to ask for permission if you are taking photos of other jewellers' work). You will see jewellery while you are out and about, and a quick sketch may spark a new idea. A notebook is really useful for cross-referencing materials – the beads that you liked on a website two weeks ago might be the perfect match for a current project. Stick swatches and magazine cuttings in your notebook, for colour matching. Finally, keep pictures of the designs you have made so that you can make them again or adapt them later.

10 Creating your own materials

If you work in polymer clay (see pages 144–147), you can create your own unique beads, drops for earrings, and pendants or brooches. Remember that the pieces that you make will look good combined with shop-bought materials, too. You can also use resins (see pages 148–149) to embellish materials that you buy and make.

Don't forget to keep looking around you for ideas – perhaps you are bored with a garment but still like its buttons; you can turn those into jewellery. Remember that you may already own some suitable materials. Sort through your old jewellery: you may find pieces that you can work into new designs.

11 Make materials your starting point

For many jewellers, the starting point for their designs are the materials they decide to work with, whether this is solely metal, beads or a combination of the two. You can choose to be wildly unconventional or stick to more conservative ideas.

12 DESIGN NOT QUITE RIGHT?

Keep working on your designs to refine them – if you aren't quite happy the first time, try again. Most threads can be re-used. Plated wires are inexpensive, and you can always use them to work up a design and then re-make it in silver wire. Even silver wires can be scrapped and sold back to the bullion dealer.

FIX IT

13 Design considerations

• **Practicality** One of the basic rules is to use the strongest construction possible for the design that you are making. This doesn't mean that you want your designs to be rigid and heavy, but you don't want to thread heavy glass beads onto a fine silk thread or use a 0.25 mm (30-gauge) wire with a chunky stone.

• **Comfort** Be practical; it is fine to create runway pieces that are impractical, but they have their limitations. Think about how your piece will be worn. Will someone's ear really take the weight of those heavy beads? Is that necklace going to damage the wearer's clothes?

• **Cost** If you are making jewellery to sell, you have to be aware of the cost of your materials so that you can work out how to make a profit. Remember to factor in the costs involved in selling the work, such as taking space at a show or the commission paid to a gallery. Cost also takes you back to your notebook – it is really helpful to keep a record of how material prices work out, and this will save you a lot of time in the future.

BEGINNERS START HERE!

14 Necklace and bracelet design

For necklaces and bracelets, the best way to start is to lay your proposed design out on your work surface and build it from the centre.

1 A piece of felt underneath your beads will give some stability. Don't plan too obsessively or start threading or wiring too soon – and remember that your design may look quite different when the components are threaded and you hold it up to check it. Don't be frightened of simplicity; let the materials speak for themselves. Work from the centre and build the design on each side.

2 Don't forget that the fastener is very important and can make or break a design. This is especially true for bracelets.

3 Not all necklaces and bracelets are made up of a single strand. Think about different shapes (a Y shape is shown here), multiple strands or an asymmetrical design. These kinds of designs are difficult to get right, but can look stunning.

TRY IT

15 USING A NECKLACE BOARD
You can use a necklace board to help you lay out your necklace. This is especially useful if you are designing with beads, since it keeps them from rolling around and helps you get the length right.

17 NOT SURE WHAT LOOKS BEST?

If you are unsure of your arrangement, try re-threading one half of your design so that you can compare both sides and decide which you prefer. Remember to check how your design will look on a person – hold it up to them and keep checking. It is a good idea to keep a mirror beside you while you work if you don't have someone to act as a model.

FIX IT

TRY IT

16 SIGNATURE FASTENING
You can incorporate a 'signature' into any necklace or bracelet – perhaps a little metalwork piece, or even a simple hammered coil – that you work in beside your fastener to stamp your identity on a piece.

BEGINNERS START HERE!

18 Earring design

There are so many options open to you when designing earrings, from hanging recycled pieces to wiring together some sparkly crystals or knitting little wire drops, as well as the beautiful metalwork pieces that you may have made. From a practical point of view, you need to think about the length and weight of your pieces. Aside from that, your designs can be as wild as you like – but always use pure metals for the ear wires.

TRY IT

19 FANCY EAR WIRE
Try creating a very simple drop, offset with a more elaborate ear wire. You can practise making fancy ear wires with cheaper wire before re-making them in a pure metal.

Finishing with crimps

The quickest way to attach a fastener is with crimps. These are small metal tubes, either ridged or plain, that come in many different sizes. They are designed to be squeezed onto threads or beading wires to hold them in place. Use a size of crimp that is appropriate for the thickness of thread that you are working with.

There are now crimps in most finishes to co-ordinate with your designs. Think about whether you prefer ridged or plain ones. Plain crimps can be folded over after you have squeezed them so that they become even smaller. Ridged crimps have the advantage of usually being fairly easy to remove if you need to make a change. If you can, it is good to work a small bead on either side of your crimp to give a professional finish.

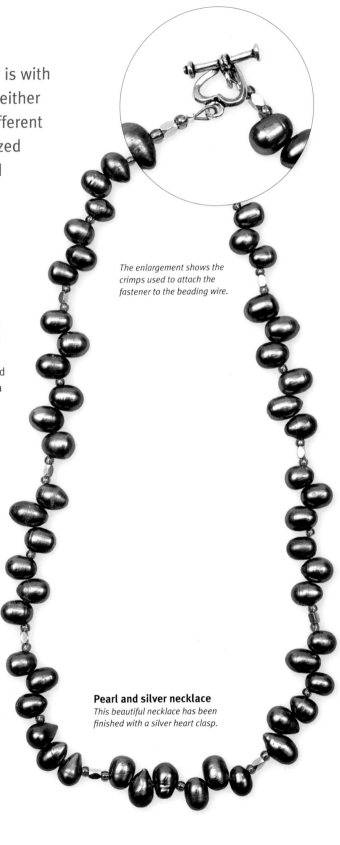

The enlargement shows the crimps used to attach the fastener to the beading wire.

Pearl and silver necklace
This beautiful necklace has been finished with a silver heart clasp.

FIX IT

20 **ADJUSTING THE LENGTH FOR A NECKLACE**
If you are unsure of the exact length that you need, because you want to be able to wear your necklace at different lengths or are making it for someone else, you can always finish it with a piece of chain at one end and a hook or a trigger clasp at the other end, to make it adjustable.

21 Fixing a fastener with crimps

If you are going to work with a lot of larger crimps, it is worth getting a good pair of crimping pliers. For small crimps and lighter threads and beads, you will be fine with chain-nose pliers.

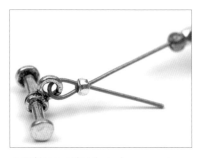

1 Making sure that the end you are not working on is secure (you can use tape to fix it to your work surface), place the crimp on the thread after the last bead at the end you are working on. Then take the thread through the fastener and back through the crimp.

2 Squeeze the crimp firmly with chain-nose or crimping pliers.

3 Test with your finger and thumb to make sure that you can't move the crimp.

4 Repeat at the other end of the work, making sure that you haven't threaded things so tightly that your work is too stiff. Either work the ends of the thread back into the beads, or cut them off close to the crimp.

22 CRIMP IS IN THE WRONG PLACE

If you have put your crimp in the wrong place and you are working with ridged crimps, or flat crimps that haven't been folded over, you can often remove them by squeezing in again from the sides after they have been flattened. Never try to use the crimps again.

FIX IT

TRY IT

23 NO CRIMPING PLIERS?

If you don't have a pair of crimping pliers, you can use flat-nose pliers instead. They will give you a secure crimp, but it will be square with corners that may be sharp, so be careful.

TRY IT

24 SMARTENING UP CRIMPS

There are many ways to make crimps look smarter. For example, you can buy crimp covers designed to be gently pressed over the crimp. If you are working with flat crimps and crimping pliers, you can use the tops of the pliers to fold the crimp back on itself.

Finishing with knots

Using crimps is the quickest way to attach fasteners, but knots are just as effective and can also become a part of your design. They are particularly useful if you are working with thicker threads and don't want to have large crimps showing. They are also excellent for those with metal allergies.

Red quartz necklace
Red quartz beads threaded on a thick polyester thread and knotted onto the T-bar fastener.

25 Fixing a fastener with knots

Some threads will be too thick for crimps to be used, so you may want to use knots instead. Always remember to give yourself plenty of thread to make the knots.

1 Making sure that the end you are not working on is secure (you can use tape to fix it to your work surface), make a simple overhand knot in your thread at the end you are working on and place a needle into this knot.

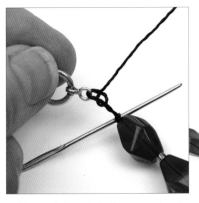

2 Now work through the fastener and start to make three or four more overhand knots between this and the first knot that you made.

3 Put the thread through the eye of the needle that you left in the knot.

26 SLIPPERY THREAD

If you are working with very slippery thread, try adding a drop of glue to the last knot. Do this carefully, as you don't want to spoil any of your beads with glue.

FIX IT

4 Now you can pull it through tightly – your knots should be secure.

TRY IT

27 THINKING ABOUT GIMP?

Gimp is a fine coiled-metal tube, which was traditionally placed over the thread where it went through the fastener to add extra strength. It is unlikely to be necessary with modern threads, but you might want to experiment with it to achieve a particular look.

Knotting between beads

Traditionally, bead necklaces were made with knots between the beads. This was done partly so that the beads didn't rub against each other and get damaged, but mainly because the threads used in the past were not as strong as they are now, since the discovery of synthetics. If a knotted necklace broke, only one bead risked being lost.

Knotting is a good skill to learn, because it will enable you to mend old necklaces, especially pearl necklaces, which need to be re-strung regularly as their enzymes keep working against the threads. Also, knotting is an extra skill that you can incorporate into your designs for aesthetic reasons. For example, it provides a way of adding extra length when using a small number of beads or stones. When knotting, always allow plenty of thread length: the knots can use up to three times the length of the finished necklace.

28 Working simple overhand knots

When working with thread, you should always use the thickest thread that you can comfortably get through your beads. Be generous with the length of thread that you allow. You will need the extra length to make the knots and it is also good to allow extra in case your thread frays a little and you want to trim off the end.

29 BEADS NOT SLIDING?

If your beads aren't sliding onto the thread easily, you can coat the thread in beeswax to help. No beeswax? Try lip balm! You could also try holding the needle from both sides and pulling it back towards the bead.

FIX IT

1 Measure plenty of thread and leave a good length at one end to attach the fastener. Add a bead and hold it in place with a piece of tape. If you are sure of the length, you can add one side of the fastener at the start. Make an overhand knot and slip a needle into it.

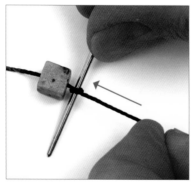

2 Use the needle to draw the knot towards the bead.

3 Start to pull out the needle while you use your fingers to keep pushing the knot towards the bead. You want the knot to sit neatly next to the bead, but not too tightly. Add the next bead and knot again. Continue in the same way.

30 Working full knots

If you want to be more adventurous, you can try full knots; these are very useful if you have beads with larger holes.

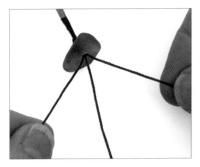

1 Start as you did before, but work three strands of thread through the beads. Again, remember to allow plenty of length – up to three times the length of the finished necklace. You'll find the process easier if you tape your work to the work surface.

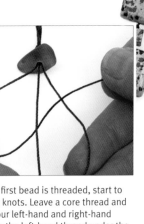

2 Once the first bead is threaded, start to make the knots. Leave a core thread and work with your left-hand and right-hand threads. Take the left-hand thread under the core thread and over the right-hand thread.

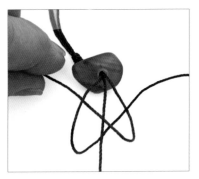

3 Take the right-hand thread over the core thread and under the left-hand thread. Pull the knot towards the bead, trying to pull down the core thread as you do so.

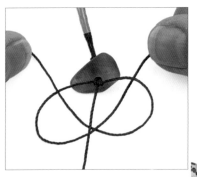

4 Then reverse the movement – left-hand thread over the core and under the right-hand thread, right-hand thread under the core and over the left-hand thread.

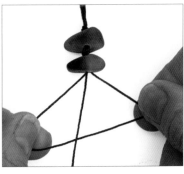

5 Take all the threads through the next bead and continue with the knots.

The knots between the beads will create flexibility and ensure that the necklace hangs well.

Dalmation jasper necklace
Dalmation jasper necklace with knots between the beads. The fastener is also attached with knots.

FIX IT

31 DISAPPEARING KNOTS

If you're having trouble with knots disappearing into the beads, you can usually make knotting easier by using a bead cap or a small bead on either side of the main bead. It saves you from having to battle to make thicker knots.

32 Knots as a design feature

You can use knots as a design feature to separate individual beads or small groups of beads. You can do this either by measuring to work out the gaps or by eye.

1 Using a good strong thread and allowing plenty of length, start in the centre of the necklace and thread on the central bead or beads. Make an overhand knot on one side.

2 Make an overhand knot on the other side of the beads and slide a needle into it. Use the needle to draw the knot towards the beads. Use your fingers to tighten the knot against the beads as you slowly pull out the needle.

3 Now make another overhand knot and slide it into position, creating a gap, before you add the next beads.

4 Repeat on the other side. You can measure if you like, but your eye should be as good as that of anyone else looking at the necklace. If you continue to work on alternate sides, you will be able to keep checking that your work is even as you go.

34 Leaving threads outside of the beads

You can tie knots in many different ways to extend your repertoire of designs. This is a great way to use thick threads and beads with a mixture of different-sized holes.

1 Knot the central beads onto the middle of a triple thread, as shown opposite.

2 Add the next bead, with or without a gap, and allow one of the threads to lie beside the bead while the others go through. Now make another knot with all three threads. Continue in this way, sometimes working all the threads through the bead and sometimes leaving one thread over the bead.

TRY IT

33 WIRE SPACED NECKLACE
If you don't want to make a spaced necklace with knots, you can try making one with beading wire, using small crimps. You can make a spaced necklace with beading wire, using small crimps on either side of the beads or groups of beads.

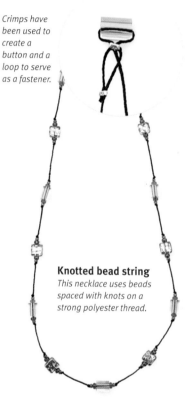

Crimps have been used to create a button and a loop to serve as a fastener.

Knotted bead string
This necklace uses beads spaced with knots on a strong polyester thread.

35 BADLY POSITIONED KNOT
If you are unhappy with the position of one of the knots, you can try to loosen or undo it with a pair of pointed or curved tweezers.

FIX IT

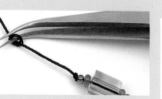

Macramé knotting to finish a necklace

This is a great way to use a few special beads and make a thick, soft, knotted braid to go around your neck. There are two variations – half-knots, which create a twisted finish, and full knots, which give a flat finish.

36 **Working half-knots**

It may be a good idea to cut some threads and practise making these knots before you start on your necklace. This will help you to learn about the different tensions.

1 When you have threaded your beads onto your core thread or threads, make an overhand knot on either side of the beads and tape one end of the work to your work surface.

2 Now add in another very long thread by knotting its centre tightly above the knot on one side of the beads.

3 Work the half-knots by bringing the left-hand thread under the core thread(s) and over the right-hand thread.

4 Tighten the knot and keep doing this, allowing the braid to twist as you work. The tension of the knotting is important, so try to keep it even as you progress.

TRY IT

37 **FLAT BEAD FASTENING**
To make a bead fastening lie flat, thread the core thread through the bead, add a very small bead and work back through the main bead.

Knotted and beaded necklace
Dichroic and furnace glass beads with half-knotted linen threads.

38 **SECURING THE LOOSE ENDS**
If you are worried that the ends will work loose, you can add a dab of superglue onto the trimmed ends to keep them secure.

FIX IT

39 Working full knots

Full knots give a lovely flat finish to your work. You'll need to concentrate to make sure you remember where you are in the sequence.

1 Start these knots in exactly the same way as the half-knots (opposite). Work the first half of the knot as before – left-hand thread under the core thread and over the right-hand thread.

2 Now bring the right-hand thread over the core thread and under the left-hand thread, and tighten the knot. These knots will create a flat braid. You'll need to concentrate on maintaining a consistent tension on the thread.

40 Button or bead fastening

You can add a fastener to your braiding to secure it in place. Alternatively, a button or a bead is a lovely way to finish it.

1 Work the core thread through a bead and face the loose end back towards your work.

2 Lay the core thread against your knotting and knot over the top of it towards the bead, finishing as close as you can to it. Pull the last knot as tight as possible.

3 Thread the ends onto a needle and work them back into the braiding before you trim all the loose ends.

41 Creating a buttonhole

Once your bead or button is in place, you need a loop for it to go through. Make sure that the loop is just large enough for the bead or button to pass through.

1 Add another small length of thread onto the core thread just below where it will line up with the button on the other side. Make a loop around your finger and the core thread and pull the end through.

2 Continue knotting until you have made enough to create a loop that will go around the button.

3 Now fold this over and continue your original knotting back towards the loop. Finish off with a tight knot, using a needle to work in the loose ends.

Knotted bracelets

You can use the techniques covered on previous pages to create knotted bracelets, such as Shamballa bracelets. You'll just need to make a few adjustments to your technique, and you can use thick threads, cords or fine leather and cotton cords.

42 Making a simple knotted Shamballa bracelet

The advantage of this bracelet design is that you can slide it over your hand and then tighten the threads once it is in place.

1 Tape one end of a long length of core thread to your work surface. Add a long thread to use for making your knots.

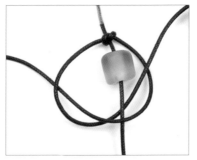

2 Thread the first bead onto the core thread, bring the knotting threads around the outside of it and make one or two full knots, as shown on page 23.

3 Thread the next bead onto the core thread, bring the knotting threads around and make another full knot. Continue in this way until you have enough beads. Remember to leave space for your fastening knots.

4 Finish by pulling the threads back through the last bead.

5 Place the ends of the core thread across each other and, using a new length of thread, fold this around them and start to make more full knots. Don't make the knots too tight, because you want your core threads to be able to slide within these knots.

6 Finish the ends by using a wire loop to thread them back into the knots for a few stitches. Cut off the loose ends and secure them with a dab of glue if you like. You can either add small beads to the ends of the core threads to keep them from pulling through the knotting, or just make a small knot at each end.

Elastic

Elastic has been revolutionized; you can now buy clear, strong elastic in different thicknesses, which is useful for making bracelets. The advantages of elastic are that you don't need to know the exact size of the wearer or struggle with fasteners.

43 Securing elastic with crimps

Using crimps to secure your elastic will create a nice neat finish, but you have to be careful that the crimps don't damage it. With both crimps and securing knots, try to create a design that will conceal them.

1 Thread your beads, then thread a large crimp onto one side. Bring the other end of the elastic back through the crimp.

2 Squeeze the crimp gently but firmly. Be careful not to damage the elastic as you do this. Clip off the ends or work them back into the beads.

44 Finishing elastic with knots

Knots give a good secure finish to your elastic bracelet, but you must get your second knot behind the first one.

1 Allow plenty of length to make your knots. Thread the beads, then bring both ends of the elastic together, make an overhand knot and pull it tight.

2 Now make another overhand knot, but work this behind the first one. A needle may help you to move the second knot over the first one. You can put a drop of glue between the knots if you want to add extra strength. Trim the ends to finish.

TRY IT

45 EXTRA STRENGTH

You can add extra strength by using two crimps with a bead in between them.

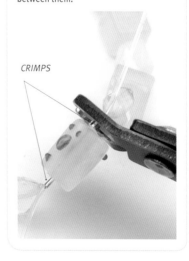

CRIMPS

Leather, cotton and rubber

Leather and cotton cords now come in a huge range of thicknesses and colours; thin-gauge cotton cord is often stronger than the leather equivalent. Suede cords are more like ribbons.

TRY IT

47 **SUEDE ENDS**
Suede cords make lovely ends to chains and necklaces – you can wrap them with wire to attach them to links in a chain or loops in beading wires (see pages 34–35.)

Beads and pendants can be threaded onto fine cords using the knotting techniques already covered in this chapter. They can be simply tied in place as described, or you can try using sliding knots, which make simple and safe necklaces for children to wear.

46 Sliding knots

This is a quick and easy way to make a necklace or pendant that you can wear at different lengths. The sliding knots are ideal for cords that have a slightly slippery finish.

Bright bead pendant
A cheap, cheerful and quick necklace – a great project to make with a child.

1 Thread on the pendant or beads you have chosen and put a knot on either side if you want to. Cross the cords over at the top of your work. Remember that you need enough length to go over the wearer's head. Pass the left-hand side of the cord over the right-hand side, then back over itself. Now put the end back through this loop and pull tightly.

2 Turn your work over and repeat to add a knot on the other side. You can trim the ends, but don't cut off too much. These knots will slide on the cord so you can lengthen or shorten the piece.

48 Using leather crimps or spring ends

This is another way to finish the ends of leather cords. When you have put the crimps or spring ends on, you can either add a fastener or a chain and a fastener to vary the length. For leather crimps, double the end of your cord and place it in the crimp. Now use chain-nose pliers to fold the sides of the crimp over the cord. Do this one side at a time and repeat at the other end of your work. For spring ends, again double the cord if you can and squeeze it into the spring end. Use a pair of chain-nose pliers to squeeze the end of the spring onto the leather.

49 Using rubber

You can get thick, solid rubber tubing, which is a very smart way of making structural-looking pieces. This can be finished with a larger version of a spring end. You can also get thinner, hollow tubing that can have a beading wire run through it and then be finished with crimps. Alternatively, try using little metal studs that work into the tube from either side to hold the rubber in place.

The little metal stud will work as a fastener; for extra security, glue one side in place.

Sea glass and rubber choker
This piece of sea glass has been decoratively wired so that it can be attached to the rubber tubing.

TRY IT

51 SPECIALIST RUBBER FINDINGS

There are specialist findings available for rubber. For example, these are ring bars that you can thread through the rubber with a central bead for decoration. One end of the bar unscrews to create the ring.

FIX IT

50 SECURING THE ENDS

If you are using spring ends, position your cord in them and squeeze the end of the spring onto the cord. If you are worried that the ends will work loose, you can add a dab of glue into the spring ends. Glue is not highly thought of in jewellery making, but it's better to be safe than sorry.

TRY IT

52 FULL LEATHER KNOTS

You could use the full knots shown on page 23 with leather cords for a bracelet or necklace fastener.

Coils and discs necklace
*Discover ways to use wire coils decoratively,
using tip number 80 on page 39.*

CHAPTER TWO:

Using wire

Wire is a wonderful material with which to bridge the gap between threading and metalwork. You can work with all kinds of wires without having to anneal them, solder them or use chemicals. In essence, you can still work on your kitchen table – as long as you have good light to work with.

Tools and materials

You will need three basic tools to master the essentials of working with wire. However, once you have learned the basics, there is a huge selection of other tools that you may find very useful.

53 Wireworking essentials

The tools that are listed below are the ones that you will have to equip yourself with. You need them to form loops, press in ends of wire and, of course, cut off the ends of your wires. There will be many variations of these essentials that you will add if you do a lot of wirework.

Remember to think of your safety, too. Be careful as you cut off small ends of wire – you may want to wear safety glasses.

• **Round-nose pliers** Choose pliers with short, neat noses so that you will feel in control of your work. Neat ends to your pliers will also enable you to make nice, small loops.
• **Chain-nose pliers** Also called snipe-nose pliers; you want to choose pliers with short, neat noses with smooth insides.
• **Flush wire cutters** Short, pointed ends will help you to get in close to your work and make neat cuts.

For some designs, you will find that a larger pair of round-nose pliers is helpful. It is also good to have some small files on hand as you start to learn more wireworking techniques.

ROUND-NOSE PLIERS

CHAIN-NOSE PLIERS

FLUSH WIRE CUTTERS

54 Use the right tool for the job

Wire cutters need looking after to keep them in top condition. Never use your best ones to cut beading wires (nylon-covered steel threads) or wires that are larger than 1mm (18 gauge) in diameter. Use an old pair to cut beading wires or, if possible, buy a special beading wire cutter; this will save you money in the long run. Try to keep a separate, heavier pair of wire cutters for cutting thicker wires.

55 Wire hardness

Think carefully about the wires that you choose. Hard wires are difficult to manipulate if you are working without heat. Soft wires are good when you are working with heavier gauges that you want to form into dramatic shapes. Remember that you can often hammer wires to harden them at a later stage. For the most basic techniques, such as closed loops, try working with a half-hard wire, especially while you are learning.

56 Getting to grips with wire

There is now a huge range of wires that you can choose from for your jewellery designs – but where to begin?

• Start by working with a good practice wire, such as a silver-plated wire, which is inexpensive but looks good.
• One of the easiest wires to work with is a 0.6-mm (22-gauge) silver-plated wire. This is silver plate on copper and has good flexibility, but it is not too soft when you work with it.
• Copper wires and coloured wires can also be good choices to start with. Experiment with different types of coloured wires to see how stable the plating is.

57 Know your wire gauges

Choosing your wire is complicated by the fact that there are two different sets of measurements. In the U.S. the width is specified by gauge (AWG), while in the UK diameters are given in millimetres.

The chart to the right shows you the two sets of measurements that are most commonly used. The very fine diameters – the higher gauges – are mostly used for decoration or specialist techniques such as knitting.

AWG	MM
38	0.1
34	0.15
32	0.2
30	0.25
28	0.3
26	0.4
24	0.5
22	0.6
21	0.7
20	0.8
19	0.9
18	1
16	1.2
14	1.5
12	2

In addition to gold- and silver-plated wire, you can also get hold of a wide variety of coloured metal wires.

TRY IT

58 USING STERLING-SILVER WIRE
Once you have mastered the basic techniques of working with wire, you may want to try working with sterling-silver wire – especially if you are making ear wires, which need to be in a precious metal. Ask for half-hard wire in the medium diameters such as 0.6mm (22 gauge). This will feel similar to the silver-plated wire that you have practised with.

59 Save up your scraps

Always remember to collect your scraps of silver wire and chain. These can be sold back to the bullion dealer. As precious-metal prices mostly go up over time, you should get a good price for your scrap.

TRY IT

60 USING PLASTIC-COVERED PLIERS
If you are working with coloured wires that mark easily, try experimenting with pliers that have plastic-covered noses. These pliers are also very good for straightening ends of wire.

Ready-made findings

The term 'findings' refers
to fasteners, ear wires and
studs, crimps, spacer bars
and many other items. In short,
they are all the 'nuts and bolts'
of jewellery making. Here we show
you some of the ready-made findings
available and begin with the wirework
loops you need for attaching your findings.

Beads on brass chain
*Ready-made head pins are
finished with simple loops
to link small drops of
beads into a chain.*

The quality of your work will be judged in part on the kind of findings that you use.
Many people now have metal allergies, so using pure metals is a good idea,
especially for ear wires. If you haven't made your own fasteners as part of the
design, there are many different types available from bead shops and websites.
You can decide on the finish and the style that works for your design.

61 Making simple loops

BEGINNERS START HERE!

To get started with a very simple bit of
wirework, try making a pair of drop
earrings. The example here uses a head
pin, which has a flat bottom and looks
like a dress-making pin.

1 Thread your beads onto your head pin.
You will need 8mm (⁵/₁₆in) of extra wire
above the beads. If you have more than this,
use wire cutters to cut off the excess.

**62 BEADS SITTING
AWKWARDLY?**

FIX IT

If you are having trouble making the
beads you've threaded onto a piece
of wire sit well together, use small
beads to help with the articulation of
the piece. Small beads are also very
useful next to the head pin, to keep
larger beads (with large holes) from
slipping off it.

2 Place your round-nose pliers close to the
beads and bend the wire towards you by
around 45 degrees.

3 Now move your pliers to the top of the
wire and, using the tip of your pliers, roll
the wire away from you so that you are
forming a loop above the beads.

4 You may be able to do this in one smooth
movement. If you can't, take your pliers
out of the loop and re-position them. Then
turn some more so that you get a complete
loop. This is now ready to have an ear wire
attached. Repeat for the other earring.

63 Eight of the best!

Here is a selection of ready-made findings that are easy to source and will provide a good starting point for your designs. They also cater to a variety of different tastes.

Ear studs Used for pierced ears. This type has a small loop, so you can add your own drops to them.

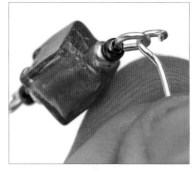

Head pins You can buy these in many different finishes and lengths and use them for drop earrings.

T-bar fastener Used as a secure fastener for either a necklace or a bracelet.

Eye pins Similar to head pins, but the ready-made loop makes them a little more versatile.

Ball and socket fastener These are new fasteners, and they can go on a necklace but are great for bracelets because they can be worked with one hand.

Hooks These are sturdy and decorative and make good necklace fasteners. They can also be linked into chain.

Trigger clasp Intended for necklaces or bracelets, they can be used with a jump ring as shown or linked straight into a piece of chain.

Ear wires These are fishhook ear wires; the bottom loop can be opened to add the pieces that you have created.

64 Linking eye pins

You can extend the basic technique of creating simple loops (opposite) by linking several eye pins together.

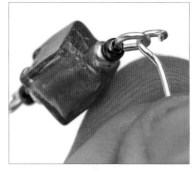

Use your pliers to gently open the loop at the end of each eye pin sideways, to enable you to link another onto it. Then close the loop.

This technique can also be used as a quick way to link drop pieces to a chain. Open the top loop of an eye pin and fit it into the links of a chain, then close the loop.

Eye pin earrings
Two ready-made eye pins are finished with simple loops and linked together.

Creating closed loops

An essential wirework technique to master is making closed loops. Closed loops can be used to link beads or little groups of beads together, or to work drilled metal pieces into chains. Having closed loops will make your drop earrings more secure, which is vital if you are using precious beads.

Semi-precious and glass bead necklace

Semi-precious beads wired into links of silver chain with closed loops.

Making perfect closed loops

65

This vital technique usually requires some practice, so use an inexpensive wire to start with.

1 Cut a couple of pieces of practice wire. You will usually need about 8cm (3in) more than the length of the bead or beads that you are going to use. Use round-nose pliers to make a loop in the wire about 2cm (³⁄₄in) in from the end. Use the power from the pliers to roll the wire away from you and bring it back over the longer wire.

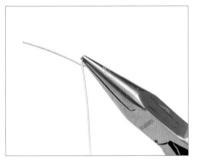

2 Now hold this loop securely with your chain-nose pliers, with the short end pointing upwards.

3 Use your fingers to bring the short end of the wire down towards the handles of your pliers.

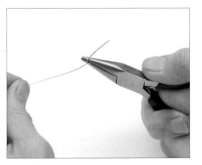

4 Bring the longer end of the wire up a little bit, so that it becomes centralized in relation to the loop. As you become more experienced with this technique, you will find that you do these two movements together with your fingers.

66 STRUGGLING WITH WRAPS?

If you are struggling to make neat wraps under your loops, try working with a longer length of wire and moving your fingers a bit farther away from the loops; you will have more control. Never try to struggle with short ends of wire: you will only make your hands sore.

FIX IT

5 Now use your fingers to wrap the short wire around the longer wire just below the loop. You will usually do two or three wraps – your choice of the number of wraps will become part of the design.

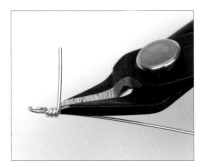

6 Use wire cutters to cut off the remainder of the short end. You will get the best results by facing the cutters towards the loop, with the cutters' smoother side lying along the wire. Take care as you cut the wire.

7 If there is any roughness left, use the chain-nose pliers to smooth the cut end of the wire back into the wraps, or use a file to smooth it. Test the smoothness with a bead in place – it may feel neat enough without extra smoothing. It is a good idea to keep practising this half of the loop until you are confident. See right for finishing a closed loop section.

67 Finishing a closed loop section

Now you are ready to make the top half of a closed loop section. Sometimes you will need only this half of the technique – for example, if you are working with a head pin or with a coil at the bottom of the wire (see page 40).

1 Place your round-nose pliers horizontally across the wire, above your bead or beads. Bring the end of the wire towards you to a 90-degree angle.

2 Now move your pliers into the angle that you have just made, and have them sitting above the bead. Start to wrap the wire around the top nose of the pliers, curving it away from you with your fingers.

3 Bring the wire down and around the pliers, then change the position of the pliers a little so that you can see the loop you have created.

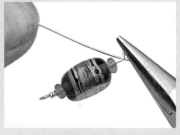

4 Hold this new loop with your chain-nose pliers and slightly adjust the position of the wire so that you have a neat loop.

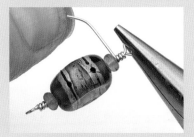

5 Bring the wire down towards the handle of your pliers and wrap back down towards the bead. Your aim is to fill the space – but you shouldn't try to wrap too tightly, since you need space for your cut end.

6 Cut off the remaining end of wire with your wire cutters. Face the smooth side of the cutters in towards your bead and cut neatly. Use a file to smooth out the end of the wire if necessary.

Jump rings will add movement.

Central section

TRY IT

68 **MAKING THE LINKS A DESIGN FEATURE**

As linked sections can be a little stiff, try using a design that makes the most of this. For example, you could make a Y-shaped necklace with a hanging central section.

1 Make your central section first with a larger top loop. Then you can work two new sections into this loop and work up both sides of the necklace.

2 To soften the line of a necklace, try using a few jump rings among your links to give a little more movement.

TRY IT

70 **GETTING THE LENGTH RIGHT**

When you are measuring pieces of wire for closed loops, always start by cutting just two lengths. Then, when you have made the first closed loop, you can see what length you actually needed and adjust the length of the second piece before cutting more.

If you are creating lots of closed loop pieces, always remember to keep a marker length, especially if you are working with sterling-silver wire and you really want to avoid waste.

69 **UNEVENLY SIZED LOOPS?**

FIX IT

If you are worried about having loops of all different sizes, you can mark your pliers with a felt-tip pen to remind you where to position the wire along the nose to get uniformly sized ones. Always use your pliers to help you measure.

When you are making the space for your wraps at the top of a closed loop, pop your pliers onto the bottom wraps to see how much space you need to create there, too.

71 A simple method for linking closed loops

Once you have mastered closed loops, you will want to start linking them together. You can make simple bracelets and chains by just working the closed loops together. However, remember that your work will become very stiff if individual sections of beads are too long. If you forget to connect the loops as you work, it is possible to link them in from either side. However, it is much easier to link as you go.

1 Make your first closed loop section, as shown on page 35. Now create the first loop on your second piece of wire. Open this loop slightly and place the first section in it.

2 Use your chain-nose pliers to hold the loop, keeping the first section out of the way as you make the wraps beside your loop. Finish this section as before and continue with your chain, joining it together as you work.

72 Making a closed loop to hang a pendant

You can use a straightforward closed loop to hang anything that is drilled up the middle. All you have to keep in mind is the size of the thread or chain that you want to hang your pendant on. You will probably need the top loop to be wider than the bottom one. Try making the loop with a wider part of your pliers.

TRY IT

73 USING CLOSED LOOPS IN DIFFERENT WAYS

If you are hanging a piece that is drilled close to the top, also try making a loop in the wire that you will open sideways to thread through the hole. Then make the wraps.

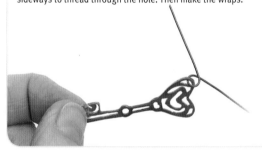

FIX IT

74 NOT SURE WHICH WAY YOUR LOOPS SHOULD FACE?

In most chains, or to hang a piece from a chain, the loops should face in the same direction. But if you are creating a chain with a central hanging section, you will want the loops to face in opposite directions. Try holding your work with two pairs of pliers and gently twisting to change the direction of the loops.

Working with chain

Mixing closed loops with pieces of chain (see page 63) will create lovely fluid necklaces and earrings. You can add drilled pieces of metalwork, beads or groups of beads to the chains.

75 Hanging a top-drilled piece

If you want to hang a piece that is drilled through the middle or the top, you can also use a closed loop.

1 Put your wire through the hole in the piece, leaving one end longer than the other. You will need about 3–4cm (1¼–1½in) of length on the shorter end to wrap above the pendant. Smooth the ends against the piece.

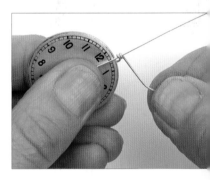

2 Wrap the shorter end above the hanging piece in the way that you would usually start a closed loop (see page 34). Make sure that you leave enough space so that you create plenty of movement.

3 Place a bead that complements the piece above the wraps and make a top loop for the pendant. Remember to make this loop the correct size for the chain that is going to be worked through it.

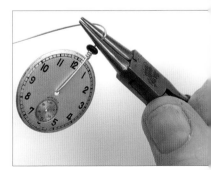

TRY IT

76 EXPERIMENT WITH SHAPES
You can mix up your chains by using just one link of a bigger chain between beaded sections.

Also, you can try working with chain in a Y-shaped necklace.

Silver chain necklace
The semi-precious and silver beads are linked into the chain links with closed loops made from silver wire.

BEGINNERS START HERE!

77 Get going with chain

Adding chain between your beads has lots of advantages; you can make a bracelet or necklace with just a few beads, plus you can create a design that you can wear at different lengths.

1 Start by planning your design, by laying components on your work surface and cutting the lengths of chain that you want to have between your sections of beads. You will probably want to have a longer length of chain to finish your necklace.

FIX IT

78 UNSURE OF THE RIGHT LENGTH?
If you aren't sure what length you want for your chain, try making it variable. If you add a longer length at one side, you should be able to find or make a fastener that will link into the chain in different positions, allowing you to vary the length.

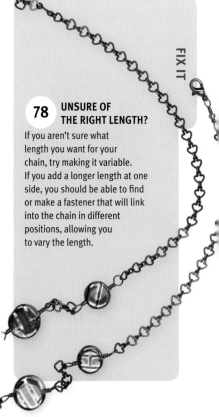

2 Begin with the piece of wire for your central section and add a piece of chain into the first loop, then make the first wraps (see pages 34–35). Add your bead or beads and make the second closed loop, adding another piece of chain before you wrap the second loop.

3 Now you can add a new wire into the piece of chain on one side, and wrap that loop. Add the beads and finish this section, remembering to add another piece of chain before you close the loop. You can work in this way up both sides of your necklace. Finish with more chain and a fastener.

Making simple findings

By adding some more techniques to your repertoire, you can make your own findings. This will enable you to match your fastener exactly to the wire that you have been using. (If you make one in the same wire, it will be a perfect match.) There is also great satisfaction to be had from being able to produce all that you need from pieces of wire and a few beads.

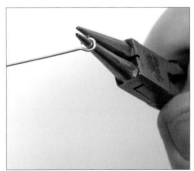

80 USING COILS DECORATIVELY
Coils can be used as decorative pieces to hang from a necklace or earrings.

Matching wire
The same wire has been used for the coils and for hanging the buttons and beads – this brings cohesion to the design.

BEGINNERS START HERE!
79 Basic eye pin

Making your own eye pin will give you freedom to create something that works perfectly with your design, because you'll be able to vary the length and thickness of the eye pin.

Double coil choker
Double coils of wire create an extra feature and add drama to the design.

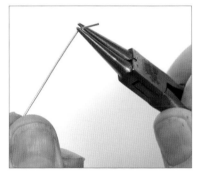

1 You can make a very simple eye pin with a loop. Place your round-nose pliers onto a piece of wire about 8mm (⁵⁄₁₆in) from the end. Bend the wire towards you.

2 Now move your pliers to the tip of the wire and use them to roll the wire away from you until you have formed a neat loop.

Making custom
81 eye pins

As you get more used to working with wire you will be able to create coils, heart shapes, stars – all sorts of clever designs that will make a decorative eye pin.

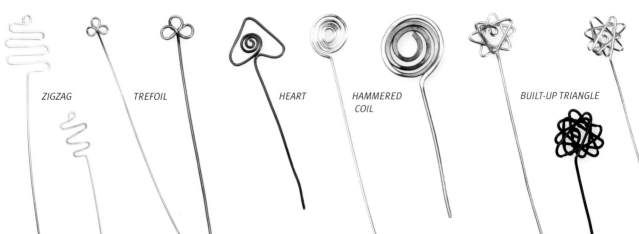

ZIGZAG   TREFOIL   HEART   HAMMERED COIL   BUILT-UP TRIANGLE

82 Making a coil eye pin

With a few variations on the basic method of making closed loops (see pages 34–35), coils can be made for both decorative and structural uses.

1 To make your first coil, cut a piece of wire, allowing plenty of length while you practise. Put your round-nose pliers against the tip of the wire and try to make the neatest loop that you can.

2 Now hold this loop with your chain-nose pliers and use them to gently roll the loop along the curve of the wire, so that you start to build a coil. You will also be feeding more of the wire onto the coil with your other hand.

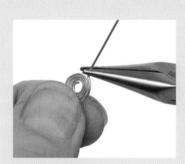

3 When you have the size that you want, or if the coil is starting to go out of shape, use the chain-nose pliers to bend the rest of the wire away from the coil. You can now add beads and finish the top with a simple loop (see page 32) or a closed loop.

83 Texturing coils

Adding texture to your coils adds another creative dimension to them, and is easy to do. You will need a hammer, a steel block and a towel to put underneath the block to dampen the sound and protect your work surface.

TRY IT

84 USING COILS AS SPACERS

You can adapt the coil technique to create a double coil that can be used as a spacer in your designs.

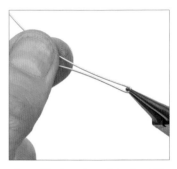

1 Start with a long piece of wire, bend it in half, then make the neatest loop that you can with the folded end.

2 Using your chain-nose pliers, start to coil the double wire, trying hard to keep it all in shape.

3 Finish by flicking out one side of the wire, then coiling a little farther and flicking out the other end of the wire. Hammering the centre of the coil will strengthen it.

85 Making a double hook

You can add beads to the hooks that you create, or wrap their centres with wire. You will be able to progress towards using thicker soft sterling wire to make heavy decorative hooks for larger designs. Refer to page 42 for the S-shaped hooks and big coil hooks.

1 Make the first half of a closed loop as shown on page 34, but use a much longer length of wire. Put a small bead onto the wire above the wraps. Now fold the wire that you have left back onto itself, using round-nose pliers. The fold will usually need to be about 3–4cm (1¼–1½in) from the bead, but this does depend on the scale of your design.

Key chain
This double hook has been worked into the chain and the small beads can coordinate throughout.

2 Use chain-nose pliers to hold the doubled wire together just above the bead, then wrap the free end of the wire around the other end.

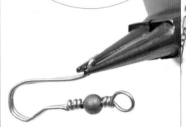

3 Finish the wraps above the bead as you would for a normal closed loop. Then, using the widest part of the round-nose pliers, bend your doubled wire to create a curved hook shape.

4 Finally, flick up the end of the hook.

86 Making a double eye

You may only need a hook if you are going to work it into a chain on one side, or a jump ring, but it also looks great if you have a matching 'eye' to complete your fastener.

1 Allowing extra wire, start your closed loop in the normal way (see page 34). Add a bead and start to make the second half of the loop. While you are making the loop above the bead, keep moving your pliers so that you can wind the wire around them twice.

2 Hold this double loop carefully with your chain-nose pliers and wrap the remainder of the wire back towards the bead. Finish off in the usual way.

Glass bead bracelet

Another version of a large silver wire hook, again based on the coil technique, and used to fasten a bracelet.

FIX IT

90 **TROUBLE HOLDING THE DOUBLED LOOP?**

If you find it hard to hold the doubled loop with your chain-nose pliers without spoiling the wire, try leaving the loop on your round-nose pliers and wrapping below them.

TRY IT

87 **MAKING A LARGE, DRAMATIC HOOK**

If you want a visually exciting hook for your necklace, try working it in a soft sterling-silver wire with a thickness of 1.2mm (16 gauge). This will be soft enough for you to work without needing to anneal it, as long as you use sturdier tools than your usual pliers and cutters. Once you have made the shape that you want, you can put it on a block and hammer it. It will then become hard enough to remain sturdy while in use.

88 **Adapting hooks for necklaces**

You can adapt the technique for making ear wires (opposite) to make simple hooks for necklaces. Try working in a heavier wire (1mm/18 gauge) to create a sturdier hook.

1 File and roll one end of your wire and make the curve around a pen.

2 You can cut and file the other end of the hook, or file it and then roll this end tightly. You can decorate this hook as well.

89 **S-shaped necklace hook**

Here is another idea for making a necklace hook. You can decorate it with beads that correspond to the rest of the piece and wrap it with a matching wire.

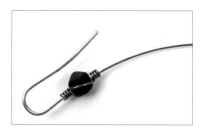

1 Bend your wire around the fat part of round-nose pliers or a ballpoint pen, then decorate the middle of the wire above the curve.

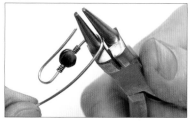

2 Make another curve in the other direction on the other side of the decoration.

3 Trim both ends, file, then roll them to finish the hook.

91 Making ear wires

The ear wires shown here are called 'fishhook' ear wires. Once you can make these, you will be able to create your own designs using different shapes and sizes.

1 Cut your piece of wire, file one end, then use your round-nose pliers to roll a small loop in this end.

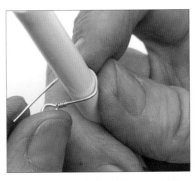

2 You can now add a bead if you would like, or wrap a small piece of wire above this loop for decoration. Bend your wire around a round ballpoint pen or similar to create a suitable curve in it.

TRY IT

92 EXPERIMENT WITH THE DESIGN
You can let your imagination run free by making your ear wires bigger or longer than usual. You can also work patterns into the wire or decorate them with beads and wires.

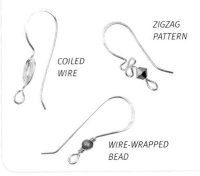

COILED WIRE

ZIGZAG PATTERN

WIRE-WRAPPED BEAD

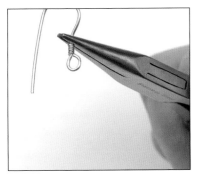

3 Use your pliers to straighten the wire a little above the loop and below the curve.

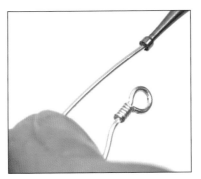

4 Cut the wire to the length that you like to have going through your ear, then flick the end up a little. Use a cup burr or file to smooth the end of the wire until it is safe to go through your ear.

5 Finally, to make the ear wire stronger, gently hammer the edge of the curve. This will also look more professional. Repeat for the other ear wire.

93 NOT SURE WHICH WIRE TO USE?
- For most drop earrings, 0.6-mm (22-gauge) wire will be strong enough.
- You may prefer slightly thicker 0.8-mm (20-gauge) wire for drop earrings.
- Most scrolls for the backs of ear studs fit onto 0.8-mm (20-gauge) wires, or look out for 0.7-mm (21-gauge) wire, which should also work.
- Remember that you will need sterling silver or gold for ear wires. Ask for half-hard wire, which will be most like the plated wire you practised with.

FIX IT

94 Coiled ear studs

You can adapt the coil technique shown on page 40 to make a very simple but pleasing ear stud. Practise using plated wire, but remember to change to a precious-metal wire when you are confident enough to make the actual piece.

Double drop earrings
Coiled ear studs with a Venetian bead drop.

1 Cut a piece of wire and bend a 90-degree angle in it about 2cm (¾in) from one end. Place your round-nose pliers against this angle and wrap the long end of the wire around the tip of them.

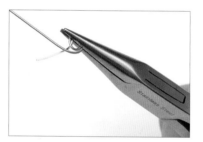

2 Hold this little loop with your chain-nose pliers and start to build a coil.

3 When the coil is large enough, cut the wire so that you just have an end left to loop back against the coil. You can hang a drop of beads from this loop.

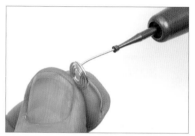

4 Cut the short wire so that it is the length that you like to have through your ear, and smooth the end with a cup burr or file. Repeat for the other stud. You will need to buy scrolls to hold the studs in place.

BEGINNERS START HERE! 95 Making jump rings

Jump rings are metal rings used for linking or attaching various elements of a jewellery piece. This method allows you to create many jump rings in one go.

1 Leaving a tail at one end of your wire so that you have something to hold onto, wrap the wire around something that is smooth, round and not tapered.

2 Make plenty of wraps so that you will have lots of jump rings. Make a mark for where you will cut.

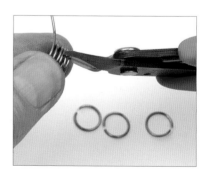

3 Slide the wraps off the former. Start to clip along the mark with a sharp pair of wire cutters.

Turkish mail bracelet
Sarah Austin has used enameled copper jump rings to create this intricate bracelet.

FIX IT

98 **KEEPING IN SHAPE**
Always open and close jump rings sideways, so that they don't lose their perfectly round shape.

1 Use a pair of chain-nose pliers in each hand and open your jump ring with a sideways movement.

2 Drop in the pieces that you want to link and use another sideways movement to close the jump ring.

96 Buying jump rings

If you don't want to make your own jump rings, there is a huge variety for you to choose from, either online or in bead shops. You need to be aware of the dimensions that are being referred to as you make your selection. Some jump rings are labelled with their inside diameter (ID) and some with their outside diameter (OD), shown in the diagram, right.

There will usually also be reference made to the gauge of the wire that they are made from. You will also need to consider the composition of the wire they are made from. Some wires, such as aluminium, can be very stiff and result in jump rings that are hard to close neatly.

OUTER DIAMETER (OD)
INNER DIAMETER (ID)

OD

ID

TRY IT

97 **USING A SAW TO CUT JUMP RINGS**
If you have been learning metalwork techniques, you may prefer to use a saw to cut through your jump rings. This would give a smoother edge.

TRY IT

99 **TOP-QUALITY JUMP RINGS**
A new breed of jump ring is now available, designed to close together very tightly. These are more expensive than the traditional type, but can be well worth it for special pieces of work made in expensive materials, where attention to detail and finishing make all the difference to a successful design.

100 Making chain mail – double or two-link chain

Chain mail (also referred to as chain maille) is a way of linking jump rings together to create decorative chains or pendants. This is a specialist technique and there are many beautiful, complex designs that can be achieved. These pages give just a taster of what is possible. You will learn these techniques more easily by working with different colours at first.

1 Start with a single ring, perhaps a slightly larger ring or a closed ring to make the closure a little stronger. Link two jump rings into this and close them securely.

2 Link two new jump rings through both of these rings and close them carefully.

3 Keep building the chain in this way until you have the length that you need.

TRY IT

101 USING A JUMP-RING HOLDER

If you are having trouble using two pairs of pliers, you can get a little gadget called a jump-ring holder to wear on one of your fingers to help with opening and closing the jump rings. If your jump rings are quite soft, you will find that you can work with your fingers and one pair of pliers. However, your fingernails may suffer!

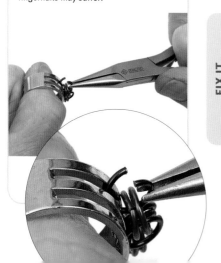

Chain-mail bracelet
This design is known as a double or two-link chain.

FIX IT

102 END LINK NEEDS SECURING?

If you are worried about the security of your end link, you might try using a soldered (closed) link or a split ring, which has a double ring of wire (like a tiny key ring), since these won't open. You can buy special pliers that make it easier to use split rings.

103 Making Byzantine chain

This pattern is quite complicated, but completing it will give you a great sense of achievement. Work with different colours while you are practising.

1 Start with a single ring in colour one (black) and add two more rings in the same colour. Now add two more rings in colour two (turquoise) and two more in colour three (purple).

2 Fold the last two (colour three/purple) back so that they sit over the first pair (colour one/black).

3 Separate the second pair (colour two/turquoise) and add two more rings (colour one/black) into the top of the colour three (purple) rings.

4 Now you will start to repeat. Add two more pairs of rings, colours two (turquoise) and three (purple), into the black rings that you added into the 'knot'.

5 Again, fold back the colour three (purple) links, separate colour two (turquoise), and add two more rings in colour one (black) into the top of the colour three rings (purple). You now have two 'knots' for your chain. You can continue in the same way as your chain builds, adding more turquoise, and so on.

FIX IT

105 GETTING MUDDLED?

If you are getting your colours muddled, lay them out in front of you with the numbers that you have given to them as a quick reminder. It is also a good idea to open your rings before you start working on a complicated project such as this chain.

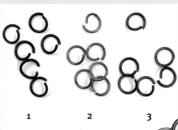

1   2   3

TRY IT

104 MIXING DESIGNS

You can try mixing the basic chain mail and Byzantine chain designs together, since they are both based on pairs of rings. You will get very different results by trying different sizes and colours of jump rings.

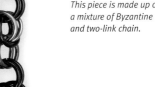

Mixed chain mail
This piece is made up of a mixture of Byzantine and two-link chain.

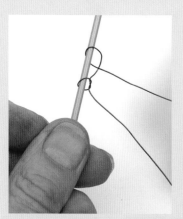

Wire bracelet
A wire-knitted bracelet with beads on alternate rows.

Knitting with wire

Knitting with wire can be fun, and it opens up all kinds of creative possibilities. You can create wonderful bracelets and cuffs, or you can experiment with smaller pieces of knitting that you can link together or use to make into earrings.

106 Getting started knitting

The first decision you may need help with is deciding which kind of wire to choose: try knitting with 0.3-mm (28-gauge) or finer wire. You can knit using either large darning needles or fine knitting needles. Cocktail sticks are often suggested, but they can be a bit too fragile and tough to use.

107 Wire knitting

You could make plain pieces of knitted wire and add beads to the edges, or try placing two sections made with different-coloured wires on top of each other. A small piece of knitting would also make a great backing for a bead or button in an earring design.

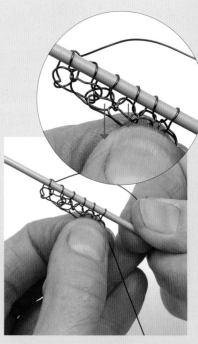

1 Create some stitches on one of your needles. You can do this by tying on the first loop, leaving a long end of wire, then looping the wire over the needle for the rest of the stitches.

2 Now start to knit in plain stitches. Try not to wrap the wire around your finger, as you might do with wool, because this will weaken it. Try to keep your knitting as loose as you can while you work.

3 The wire knitting will look very messy at first, but you can start to pull it gently into shape after a few rows.

108 Knitting with beads

Knitted wire looks wonderful with beads worked into it. You have the choice of adding beads into every row or every other row. Every row looks more opulent, but you will have a lot of beads to thread before you start knitting.

1 First you have to thread the beads that you need onto your wire. Start as you did for plain knitting, opposite, and work two rows without beads. On the third row, knit as before but move one bead up your wire and drop it into your stitch as you make it.

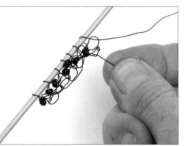

2 Continue adding your beads in this way as you knit. On your next row, you will need to decide whether you want to have beads on every row or every other row. Try to keep the knitting loose as you work.

3 Finish your knitting with a couple of plain rows to match the first two rows. Work the wire back through these stitches to finish off the knitting.

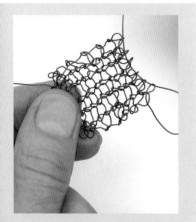

4 Work as long a piece as you need. There is no need to cast off. You will take the piece off your needle and run the loose wire back through the stitches. Work new wires into your knitting to add a clasp if you are making a bracelet.

109 NOT SURE HOW MANY BEADS YOU WILL NEED?

FIX IT

If you do a small piece of knitting as a practice piece, you will have a chance to see how it will look and be able to calculate how many beads you will need.

TRY IT

110 TAKING KNITTING FURTHER You can add more wire and beads to embellish the edges of your knitted pieces if you want to make your design more elaborate.

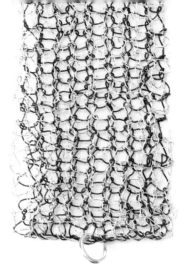

Try pulling and pushing small knitted pieces into different shapes with your fingers. In this way you can make lovely earrings or pendants.

Getting the most out of memory wire

Memory wire is a strange material, and using it falls somewhere between wirework and threading. It is a very strong coiled wire and, as the name suggests, it doesn't 'forget' its coils.

The most important thing to remember about working with memory wire is that you must use heavier cutters, or special memory-wire cutters, since it will destroy normal wire cutters. You will also need heavier round-nose pliers.

Memory-wire cutters

Coiled memory-wire bracelet
Cat's eye beads and silver spacers have been used by Allene Krueger in this coiled bracelet.

111 How you can use memory wire

Memory wire is made in different sizes and it is most suitable for rings, chokers or bracelets. It is not really possible to manipulate it; you can only make simple loops to finish it. Memory wire is good when you want to add strength and stiffness to a design; you can't use it where you want any flexibility or softness.

112 Making a coiled memory-wire bracelet

Memory wire is probably most useful for making bracelets. You can make thick bracelets using several coils.

Memory-wire bracelet
A selection of beads on a coil of memory wire.

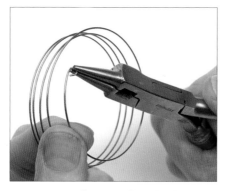

1 Cut as many coils as you will need with your memory-wire cutters. Be careful as you do so: memory wire has a nasty habit of trying to prick you. Roll one end of the wire with heavy round-nose pliers. Roll away from the curve of the wire.

2 Thread on your beads or charms. You will need to focus on beads that aren't too long. Make another loop at the other end of the wire. You won't need a fastener – it will just wind around a wrist.

113 Making a memory-wire bracelet

You can make bracelets or cuffs easily, using single strands of memory wire.

A bracelet like this will need a fastener, so start making a loop that you can work a fastener or chain into. Add your beads, trim the end of the wire with memory-wire cutters, then finish with another loop.

114 Making a double-stranded bracelet with memory wire

If you are making a double-stranded bracelet with memory wire, or an even wider one, it is a good idea to put spacer bars between each section.

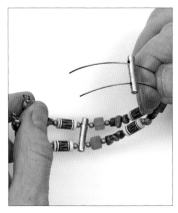

1 Cut two lengths of memory wire. Work with both lengths at the same time and make loops in the end. Now add your beads. You will get better results if you add spacer bars as you work.

2 Finish each coil of wire by making another loop with your round-nose pliers. These loops can be used to add a fastener or a small length of safety chain.

115 HAVING TROUBLE MAKING THE END LOOPS?

You can press the loops together with a pair of chain-nose pliers to close them up a bit.

FIX IT

117 READY-MADE ENDS

If you find making the loops difficult, you can buy ready-made memory-wire ends that you glue in place instead.

FIX IT

TRY IT

116 ADDING MORE

You can add to your double bracelets by wrapping a decorative wire and possibly more beads around both strands.

18-karat gold wrap-over ring
*Understand more about the properties of gold
in tip number 126 on page 59.*

CHAPTER THREE:
Metalwork basics

This section gives you an insight into jewellery design and making with metal. It covers many aspects of the process, from understanding the properties of metals to important details such as how to set up your workspace and how to get hold of the materials you need.

Health and safety

A jewellery workshop has some potential risks to be aware of. It makes sense to keep yourself informed and stay organized to help you avoid accidents. There are also a few important items that you should have on hand in your work environment.

A first-aid kit is essential. This should contain, as a minimum:

- Plasters
- Bandages
- Antiseptic cream
- Eyewash and eyebath
- Burn spray

You should also have a fire blanket and fire extinguisher near where you are working. Always wear safety goggles when you are polishing or drilling.

118 Workshop safety tips

- Don't light your torch with a disposable lighter: if the lighter is exposed to heat, it might explode, which could cause serious burns. A gas lighter is a much safer option.
- Always store any potentially dangerous chemicals securely, especially if you are using them in your kitchen. When you're not using them, put them away out of reach or in a lockable cupboard.

- If you have a torch that requires butane canisters, make sure these are stored in a cool place, detached from the torch in case they leak.
- Always read the hazard labels on any chemicals you are using (see right).
- Never wear sandals or flip-flops in a workshop. Wear shoes to protect your feet from heavy or sharp items, or hot metal, falling on them.

GENERAL HEALTH AND SAFETY TIPS

- Work in a well-ventilated area so that any dust or fumes produced when you are working are quickly dissipated.
- Ensure your workspace is well lit; proper lighting will help with accuracy and prevent eyestrain.
- Tie back long hair and avoid wearing loose clothing or jewellery, which can get caught on equipment.
- Clean up after yourself – put chemicals, tools, and materials away after use; vibrations made from hammering or other processes can cause tools to fall off surfaces.

- Keep the floor of the work space clear of items that could cause trips or falls.
- Clean up liquid spills and dust as soon as possible.
- Don't allow children or pets into the work space.
- Have a first-aid kit at hand, in case of minor cuts and burns.

HAZARD SYMBOLS

It is a good idea to familiarize yourself with the commonly used hazard symbols, which are used to warn of dangerous materials you may encounter in a jewellery workshop.

FLAMMABLE

CORROSIVE

TOXIC

OXIDIZING AGENT

HARMFUL

EXPLOSIVE

119 Carrying out a risk assessment

Before you start making your jewellery piece, think about all the
things that might present a risk – and how you can prevent the risk or
deal with any accidents.

ACTIVITY	RISK	PREVENTION	REMEDY	DANGER LEVEL (★ TO ★ ★ ★)
Sawing	*Cutting your fingers*	• Keep fingers behind saw blades	• Antiseptic cream and plaster	★
Soldering	*Burns*	• Never pick up hot items • Make sure pieces are stable and can't fall off the work surface	• Run burnt skin under cold water	★
	Fire	• Remove flammable items before soldering	• Cover with fire blanket • Use fire extinguisher • If serious, phone fire service	★ ★ ★
Polishing	*Clothing caught in wheel*	• Don't wear loose clothing or dangling jewellery or scarves	• If badly hurt, seek medical attention	★ ★ ★
	Hair caught in wheel	• Always tie back long hair	• If badly hurt, seek medical attention	★ ★ ★
	Grit or polish in eyes	• Wear safety goggles	• Wash with eyewash	★
	Cut from metal being polished	• Hold metal firmly • Never polish chains	• Antiseptic cream and plaster • If badly hurt, seek medical attention	★ ★
Drilling	*Cut from metal being drilled*	• Clamp anything being drilled	• Antiseptic cream and plaster • If badly hurt, seek medical attention	★
	Shavings going in eyes	• Wear safety goggles	• Antiseptic cream and plaster • If badly hurt, seek medical attention	★ ★
Pickling	*Irritation to hands*	• Wear gloves	• Wash hands	★

Setting up your workshop

How you set up your workshop will depend on the amount of space you have available, the type and number of tools you have and how many different techniques you are planning to carry out.

120 Permanent set-up

The main benefit of having a separate workshop, however tiny, is that you can leave everything out when you finish working and simply pick it up again where you left off the next time you're ready to work on it. Whatever space you have, though, you will quickly fill it up, so it's good to have a plan of the layout to start with.

Lighting

Good lighting is essential for making jewellery, so you don't strain your eyes. Ideally you should have lots of natural light, which is particularly good when it comes from a skylight. If there isn't a lot of natural light, you can install overhead lighting – you can buy special daylight simulation bulbs, which give off a white light. Fluorescent lighting is not good to work with, though – it flickers, and this can be disturbing.

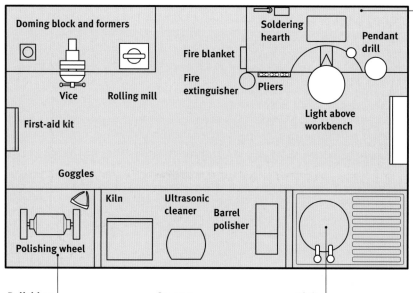

Soldering

You can either have a soldering hearth on your workbench or have a separate area for soldering if you have the space.

Seating

It is important to have your chair at the right height for the workbench, because if you spend hours in a chair that's too high, you may start to have neck and back problems. The ideal bench height is just below chest level. If you sit at a kneeling chair it is difficult to sit with bad posture, so this may help prevent back and neck problems.

Polishing

You should carry out polishing in a separate area, mainly because polishing on a wheel is extremely messy and produces a lot of fluff and dust. You can make a divider out of wood to place on either side of the polishing wheel to prevent dirt from covering everything.

Storage

It is good to have your most-used tools close at hand. To keep them organized you can hang the most useful pieces, such as saw frames and pliers, on the wall, and keep less-used tools protected inside cupboards so that they don't get damp or damaged.

Sink

If it's possible to have one, a sink is really useful in a workshop, for washing your hands or refilling the pickle, for instance. There are alternatives, though (see Fix it, page 57).

Heating

It may seem expensive to heat a workshop when you're not in it, but if your workshop is a wooden shed – as many are – during the winter months you will find that the damp may start to rust your tools. An oil-filled radiator is a good way of maintaining a low background heat to help prevent this.

Flooring

This may seem obvious, but don't have a floor covering that is flammable (for example, carpeting) or a floor that has lots of gaps (such as between floorboards), or you may lose pieces of wire and tiny stones and beads in the gaps.

121 Temporary set-up

If you can't have a dedicated workshop, you can have a makeshift workspace at your kitchen table. Keep all your tools in a handy box, preferably with compartments, so that they're easy to access. Any chemicals or butane canisters should be kept securely stored when not in use.

Clearing up
If you are working in a kitchen where food is prepared, it's very important to wipe down surfaces and floors carefully to make sure you haven't left any little bits of metal behind. Store all your chemicals and butane securely and never where food is stored.

Soldering
You can use a portable butane gas torch for soldering. The safest place to solder in a kitchen is at a metal draining board, because the metal is not flammable and you are next to a water supply. (Do tie any nearby curtains out of the way first, though.) To store the torch, remove it from the butane canister, so that it can't leak.
It's also a good idea to put a protective floor covering down underneath where you are soldering, in case anything hot falls onto the floor.

Floor protection
Wooden or metal sheet.

Lighting
For extra lighting where you want to work, you can buy magnifying lamps that clamp onto the table (the magnifying function may be useful, too).

Fire extinguisher

Slow cooker

First-aid kit

Storage box

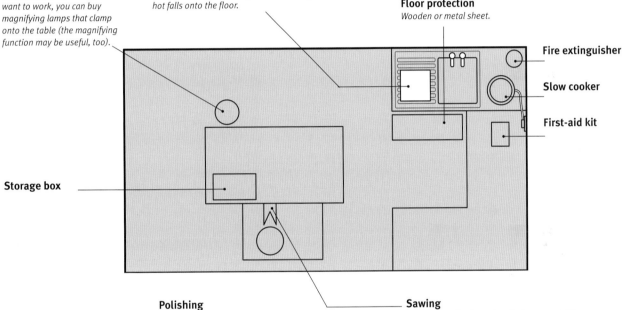

Polishing
For a temporary set-up, a hobby drill with special attachments works well for polishing. Alternatively, you could use a barrel polisher, which doesn't produce any mess.

Sawing
You can attach a loose bench pin to your table with a G-clamp. You may want to protect your table from damage with a scrap piece of wood between it and the clamp.

122 SINK ALTERNATIVE
FIX IT
If you don't have a sink in your workshop, you can set up a water container with a tap at the bottom, of the type used for camping. Place it on a work surface, with a bucket underneath to collect the waste water.

TRY IT

123 MAKE YOUR OWN TEMPORARY WORKBENCH
One option for a temporary workbench is to make one that folds away. For example, you could adapt a bench intended for woodworking. Cut out a thick piece of plywood to fit the workbench, with a semi-circular cut-out, and fit a bench pin onto it; when it's not in use, it can simply be folded away. Woodworkers' benches are great to use, because they are designed for sawing and hammering on and are very sturdy.

Which metal to use?

Most metals can be used in some way in jewellery design and manufacture, from traditional silver and gold to less-used metals such as aluminium and bronze. Each metal has its own specific properties that you can take advantage of and combine with those of other metals and materials to create unique pieces of jewellery.

When you are choosing a metal to use for a jewellery design, there are many considerations that will affect your decision – including the cost, the colour of the metal, the tools you have available and the malleability of the metal. It's all about choosing the metal that is most suited to your design. Some metals, such as platinum, steel and palladium, require specialist tools or training. On the following pages, some of the more common metals for jewellery making are described.

124 Silver

Silver is an element. It has been prized for centuries for making jewellery and silversmithing objects, such as bowls and candlesticks. It is chosen for its ease of shaping and soldering, its brilliant shine and its white colour. In Ancient Egypt it was once more highly valued than gold, since it was rarer and believed to be the bones of a god.

Silver is available in different grades, depending on its purity. Grades range from nickel silver, which cannot be hallmarked, to fine silver, which is 99.9% silver.

Silver bangle
An oxidized and textured silver bangle by Lorreta Dwane.

125 Metal properties

The chart below outlines important properties that you will need to consider before finalising your jewellery design. For example, if you cannot silver solder your intended piece you will need to look into other ways of joining, such as riveting.

METAL	CAN IT BE SILVER SOLDERED?	MELTING POINT	CHEMICAL SYMBOL	COLOUR
Gold	Yes	1,064°C (1,947°F)	Au	Yellow
Silver	Yes	893°C–960°C (1,640°F–1,760°F)	Ag	White
Copper	Yes	1,979°C (3,594°F)	Cu	Brown
Bronze	Yes	1,550°C–1,850°C (2,822°F–3,362°F)	–	Brown
Brass	Yes	1,600°C–1,849°C (2,912°F–3,360°F)	–	Yellow
Aluminium	No	482°C–677°C (900°F–1,250°F)	Al	Grey
Pewter	No	254°C (490°F)	–	White
Niobium	No	2,477°C (4,491°F)	Nb	Grey
Titanium	No	1,668°C (3,034°F)	Ti	Grey

126 Gold

Gold is an element. It has been used for centuries to make jewellery because of its brilliant shine, malleability, spectacular colour and longevity. It was highly prized by the Aztecs and Ancient Egyptians, who considered it to symbolize the sun.

The high price of gold limits its use to smaller-scale pieces of jewellery. It can also be used to add decorative accents – for example, when soldered onto silver.

Gold is alloyed with other metals to create different grades, known as karats (it is graded from 8 karat up to 24 karat – the purest gold). The karat rating also depends on what country the gold comes from.

Wrap-over ring
An 18-karat wrap-over gold ring using reticulation as a surface pattern, with a tube-set faceted blue topaz.

Colours of gold

Gold comes in different colours, depending on what metals it has been alloyed with.
- White gold = gold + zinc or nickel
- Yellow gold = gold
- Red gold = gold + copper + silver
- Green gold = gold + silver

127 Copper

Copper is an element. It is not widely used for jewellery, because it can leave a green mark on the skin (although you can seal it with a varnish to prevent this). You can produce interesting colours on the surface of copper – either by heat-treating it, which produces warm reds and browns, or by using a chemical called cupra to produce a matte-green effect called verdigris. Copper can also be applied as decoration to other metals, such as silver. It is a very malleable metal that can be easily shaped and moulded with hammers and punches.

Copper necklace
This unusual copper chain by Boris Bally has been made using pennies.

Bronze pendant
This hare pendant shows the lustrous quality of polished bronze.

128 Bronze

Bronze is an alloy of copper (usually around 90%) and tin or zinc (around 10%) – the percentages can vary. Bronze is mainly used for casting, which produces durable objects. Since the Bronze Age it has mainly been used for making sculptures and medals and not so much for jewellery, apart from by the Romans. However, it is well suited to jewellery making because it doesn't leave a green mark on the skin, as copper does, and when it is polished it has an antique gold look, which can be a cost-effective alternative to gold. Bronze can be patinated in many different colours.

129 Brass

Brass is an alloy of copper (60–90%) and zinc (10–40%). It can successfully be made into jewellery, and has a bright gold colour when polished. Brass is very hard and unmalleable, but it can be successfully applied as decoration to other metals, such as silver or copper. A type of brass that contains 95% copper and 5% zinc is known as gilding metal.

Filigreed brass pendant
A patina of ammonium chloride and copper sulphate has been applied to the brass surface of Sarah Karst's pendant, to produce a luscious green colour.

130 Aluminium

Aluminium is an element. It hasn't been widely used for jewellery until recently, but is now chosen for its ability to be coloured and printed onto. This is only possible with anodized aluminium, though, which has an absorbent layer that accepts dyes. The anodized layer also toughens the aluminium. The process of anodizing requires the use of toxic chemicals, so is only suitable in a proper workshop environment, but you can buy pre-anodized sheet, which is ready to dye or print onto. This must be carefully stored away from moisture, otherwise it will degrade over time.

There are various dyeing methods, including using permanent markers to draw directly onto the surface, or drawing onto rubber stamps and printing onto the surface (see page 110). You can also use dyes to either paint onto the aluminium or dip it into. Many print-making techniques can also be applied to the aluminium to create unique and original designs.

One of the advantages of aluminium is its weight; it is very light, so you can make quite large items of jewellery that are still comfortable to wear. Aluminium can't be soldered, so riveting is the most common way of joining it, either to itself or to other metals or materials.

Mechanical aluminium brooch
This brooch by Lindsey Mann makes use of printed anodized aluminium as well as other metals and found materials.

131 Pewter

Pewter is an alloy of tin (85%), as well as copper, antimony and bismuth in different amounts. It is used to make jewellery and various other objects, and can be easily cast because of its low melting point. You can buy it as casting bars, which can be easily melted in a crucible with a butane torch. You can then pour the molten pewter into a variety of types of mould, from sand to plaster. It solidifies quickly once it is cool and can be sanded and polished to resemble silver, or left matte. Pewter can be soldered with tin solder. You can also buy it in sheet form, which is extremely malleable.

Cast pewter
This cast bee necklace from Glover and Smith demonstrates the intricate detail you can achieve using pewter casting.

132 Niobium

Niobium is an element. It has similar properties to titanium, but is easier to work with. It is extremely hard and tough, but also lightweight. It can be sawn, although it must be lubricated during sawing and also when it is drilled. The blades and drill bits will be worn out quite quickly because of its hardness. It can also be shaped by doming or folding. Like titanium, it can't be soldered, so it must be riveted to join it. An important property of niobium is that it is hypoallergenic – you can buy earring wires made from it, which are good for people with metal allergies.

It is possible to create rainbow colours on the surface of niobium, which can be very useful in jewellery design. Unlike with titanium, there is no need for chemicals to etch the surface first – the colours can be created with a torch, which can start at a temperature of 338°C (640°F). The first colour to show itself is yellow, but colours can range from blue-purple through to various greens.

133 Titanium

Titanium is an element. It has only fairly recently been used for jewellery. It is not an easy metal to work with because of its extreme strength and very high melting point. In its natural state it is a silvery to dark grey, but it is often chosen for its ability to take on an array of rainbow colours.

Care must be taken with titanium when you use any technique that produces a lot of friction, such as high-speed drilling. This can cause spontaneous combustion.

Anodized titanium pendants
This series of cloud pendants, made by Vanessa Williams, was created using hydraulic press-formed titanium.

Buying metal

Metal can be bought in different profiles and sizes, and in wire and sheet form. It is useful to be aware of this when you are designing jewellery, so that you can consider designing around these sizes and shapes.

It's worth shopping around and comparing prices when buying metal, although precious metals (bullion) have a set price per gram, which changes daily on the stock market.

To buy precious metals such as silver or gold, you will need to go to a specialist metal supplier. Base metals are usually available from a different type of supplier – for example, a model-making supplier: they will stock materials such as brass and copper sheet, rod and tubing. However, some bullion companies also stock certain base metals.

Sheet metal
From left to right: aluminium, niobium and titanium.

136 Mokume gane sheet

Mokume gane can be bought as a ready-made sheet. This is a Japanese decorative metal technique, which is very time-consuming and difficult to produce – it's a mix of copper and silver, or other metals, which are soldered in layers and rolled very thinly to create a kind of two-toned woodgrain effect. Mokume gane sheet can be used to decorate pieces of jewellery.

134 Ordering sheet metal

Most metals are available to buy as sheets, in thicknesses measured by gauge (U.S.) or in millimetres (U.K. and Europe). You have to be careful when ordering metals by gauge thickness, because there are many different systems for different metals. However, it is always the case that the larger the number, the thinner the metal. The following chart works for steel and most non-ferrous metals such as brass and copper.

GAUGE	MM
14	1.8
16	1.5
18	1.2
20	0.9
22	0.7
24	0.6
26	0.5

137 Blanks

You can buy ready-cut metal shapes – discs are the most commonly available – in different diameters and thicknesses. These come in gold, silver, copper and brass. You can also buy other pre-cut shapes: blanks for enamelling in copper and silver, shaped cufflink blanks and various other shapes such as hearts and stars, usually in copper or silver.

135 Ethical concerns

Many jewellery makers are concerned with where their materials have come from. Mining for metal is often done in developing countries, where workers' conditions and pay are poor. Mining can also have adverse conditions on the environment – for example, by polluting rivers with chemicals used in the mining process. These issues have sparked a recent campaign for jewellers to buy fair-trade silver and gold, which helps guarantee fair conditions and pay for the workers who produce it.

138 Ordering wire

Wire comes in different thicknesses and profiles, but not all metals will come in all of the different profiles and dimensions. For example, you can buy silver round wire soft, fully annealed (heated to make the metal more malleable), half-hard or hard. You would use soft wire to make shapes in if it was to be soldered onto something or heated, as this anneals it anyway. Hard is used if you want a non-bendy wire – for instance, to make brooch pins. Half-hard can be used for making ear wires, since you need to be able to bend the wire easily to make the shape, but you don't want them to bend while they are being worn. Most other profiles of silver wire are available only as soft, fully annealed.

Wire is available to buy measured by gauge (U.S.) or in millimetres (U.K. and Europe). The millimetre diameter can be very slightly larger or smaller than shown in the table (below, right). The chart (right) shows the suitability of certain wire profiles for various pieces of jewellery.

WIRE PROFILE	USES
Round	Filigree, ear wires, rings, bangles, chains, jump rings
Square	Rings, bangles
D-section	Rings, bangles
Rectangular	Rings, bangles, pendants, earrings
Oval	Rings, bangles
Bearer wire	Settings
Chenier (tubing)	Findings, settings
Gallery strip (patterned strips, mainly of silver)	Settings, decorative rings

139 Chain

You can buy many different types of chain, mainly in gold, silver, copper and plated metals. Chains are usually sold by length, which means you can easily make a non-standard length to suit your needs; you just need to add clasps to the ends.

140 Findings

Findings are ready-made fittings, designed as components for jewellery. There are many types of items, mainly in silver and gold, but also as plated metals. Examples include earring studs and wires, clasps for necklaces, jump rings (ready-made rings for attaching different elements), pendant bails, brooch fittings, cufflink fittings, tie pins and stone settings. They are all very useful for saving time if you don't want to make every single component in your jewellery design.

141 Ring and bangle blanks

You can buy complete ring and bangle shapes. These give you the basic shape to start with, if you are only interested in decorating a piece. They come in a variety of shapes and sizes – you can even get napkin rings.

GAUGE	MM
14	1.6
16	1.2
18	1
19	0.9
20	0.8
21	0.7
22	0.6
24	0.5
26	0.4

TRY IT

142 MAKE YOUR OWN COPPER WIRE

If you have unused electrical cables, you can strip the plastic coatings off with wire strippers, and underneath you will find copper wire. The thickness will depend on the type of cable you have. Using this copper wire is a great way of recycling – and saving money, too.

143 Casting grains

Casting grains are available in gold, silver and bronze. These are granules of metal that are designed to be melted and cast in a mould. (You may need specialist equipment to melt and cast some metals that have high melting points.) You can also use casting grains soldered onto a piece as decoration. Pewter comes as bars for casting, not in grain form.

Essential metalwork toolkit

When you start creating jewellery, you need to think about the sort of work you want to do. Perhaps you just want to make jewellery out of wire, or to concentrate on stone setting, for example. What you decide will influence the types of tools you will need.

For basic metalwork you don't need a large number of tools – just a few well-chosen pieces. Try to buy the best quality you can afford, since these tools will last you a lifetime, if looked after. A rule of thumb is that Swiss- or German-made tools tend to be of very high quality. The following pages cover the essentials to get you started.

144 Workbench

You can buy a solid wood workbench with drawers and a bench pin fitted. Workbenches can be expensive, but there is a wide range available; however, they all have a semi-circle cut from the front and a bench pin fitted. The most important thing about a workbench is that it is sturdy and heavy-duty. You can improvise your own out of a heavy table.

145 Bench pin

A bench pin is essential for sawing onto – this is a wooden wedge with a V-shape cut out of it. What you buy will depend on what sort of workshop set-up you have. If you have a traditional workbench, then either a bench pin will be supplied ready fitted or you can buy one and fit it yourself. Generally, bench pins are made of beech. If you are working in a temporary set-up, you can buy a bench pin that is fitted with a clamp, which also has a small steel block attached. Whichever kind you choose, all bench pins come without the V-shape cut into them, so you will need to saw it out to your own design.

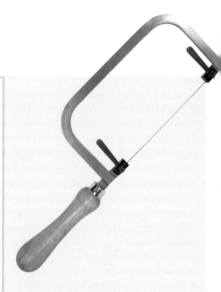

146 Saw frames

The frames of most piercing saws are of a similar design, but you can get different depths. The depth is measured from the saw blade to the back of the frame, and this affects the width of metal you can cut. Generally, for jewellery, you would use a 7.5-cm (3-in) frame. There are a few variations available – for example, you can buy an adjustable saw frame, which means you can adjust the size of the blade; there's also a Grobet saw frame, which has a patented design with a slightly different way of fixing in the blade. Also there's a new style of frame, called a Knew Concept, which is very lightweight and has a unique way of tensioning the blade, but this is more expensive than regular saw frames.

147 Files

Files are for shaping, refining and straightening metal edges. You can buy them in a variety of profiles and sizes, the most common being flat, half-round, round, triangular, square and barrette. There are needle files (small files, pictured below), full-size files and also riffler files, which have shaped ends. You can buy these separately or as a basic pack, which is usually an economical way of starting out. The most useful type of file is half-round.

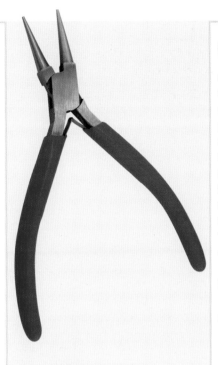

148 Pliers

Pliers are used for bending metal or wire. Most are made of steel, although some are available with nylon jaws, which protect the metal from being marked or scratched.

Flat-nose pliers

Flat-nose pliers have two flat jaws and are useful for straightening out or bending metal into angles. There is also a snipe-nose version, which has tapered flat jaws that are good for getting into smaller areas.

Round-nose pliers

Round-nose pliers (pictured above) have two round jaws, tapering to a point; these are useful for shaping wire and sheet metal into curves or coils.

149 Ring mandrels

A ring mandrel is a long, tapered, round steel tool for shaping rings or links around. Different sizes and profiles are available, but the most useful size is 40cm (16in). Smaller mandrels can be used for making stone settings, and the larger ones are used for shaping bangles on. There are also square mandrels for making square-shaped rings. You can buy ring mandrels with ring sizes on them (numbers in the U.S., letters in the U.K.); these are usually only used for sizing and not for hammering around.

150 Hammers

Hammers are usually made of steel, which is harder than silver or copper and will indent the metals you are working on. There are many different weights, sizes and shapes of hammers. The most useful kind of hammer to start with has one rounded end and one flat end, but there are also polishing, jobbing and repoussé hammers available. All have one round end and one flat end, and can be used for general hammering and planishing.

Planishing hammer

Jobbing hammer

151 Steel block

This is a heavy solid block of steel, used to hammer onto and straighten metal on. It provides a hard, resistant surface to support metal while it is being worked on, and will prevent sheet metal from distorting as it would if hit on a wooden surface.

152 Mallets

Mallets are usually rawhide or wooden. They are used to hammer metal into shape, usually onto a steel base or former. You use them when you want to shape the metal but not mark it – for example, when shaping a ring on a mandrel.

153 Measuring and marking tools

Centre punch

A centre punch is a steel pointed tool used to make a small indent – for example, to locate a drill bit to enable you to drill a hole without the drill bit slipping. You can also buy an automatic centre punch.

Scriber

A scriber is a long, thin, pointed steel tool used for scribing out designs on the metal.

Steel ruler

A steel ruler is used for measuring metal accurately and scribing against. They are usually available in 15-cm (6-in) or 30-cm (12-in) lengths.

154 Drills

There are many types of drill available to suit all pockets. The one you choose will depend on whether you only want it for making holes or if you also want to use it for stone setting and polishing.

Archimedes drill

An Archimedes drill is great if you just want to drill holes. It is very simple and cheap, and is spring loaded; you just push down on the top and then release to turn the drill bit. It is also very good if you don't like using power tools.

Bow drill

This is very traditional and simple to use – again, ideal if you just want to drill holes. It works on the same principle as the Archimedes drill, except that with this there are two pieces of cord that wind up and then unwind. This produces the centrifugal turning motion, a little like a spinning top.

Hobby drill

If you want to use attachments other than just drill bits, such as burrs, sanding and polishing attachments, and so on, there are many different types of electric hobby drill. This is a good mid-range cost option.

Pendant drill

A pendant drill is a more professional drill for jewellers, and it generally offers more precision than a hobby drill. The main difference is that you have a foot pedal to operate the drill, which leaves both your hands free. The motor hangs up on a hook and a flexible shaft hangs down. This means you hold a slim hand piece, which is suitable for tasks that require high levels of precision and concentration, such as burring or stone setting. Pendant drills are the most expensive option.

155 Torches

You will need a torch to solder with. There are many different types to suit all budgets and situations. If you are planning to set up a permanent workshop with a dedicated bench, you will want to consider getting a propane torch or a mouth-blown torch; if you are working in a temporary set-up, you can use a small, catering-style butane torch. This will limit some of the work you can do, although most small-scale soldering can be done with such a torch.

Portable butane torch

There are different versions on the market – some use butane/propane camping gas-type canisters and some are very small torches that can be filled with lighter refill bottles. Be very careful to remove lighter fuel and gas lighters from the place where you are soldering, because if they are heated they will explode.

Propane torch

Propane torches are run from larger bottles of propane gas and usually have changeable burner heads, which means that you can carry out both small-scale and larger areas of soldering. Another advantage is that a lot of the components can be replaced.

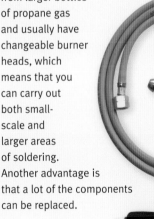

Mouth-blown torch

This is the most traditional form of the jeweller's torch. It also runs on propane gas, but the difference is that you have a length of rubber tube to blow into to regulate the amount of oxygen in the flame, which affects its temperature.

156 Silver strip solders

There are different grades of solder available. These come in silver strips of different widths, and it's important to keep different solders clearly labelled in separate containers so that you can see what you are using.

SOLDER	MELTING TEMPERATURE
Enamelling	730°C–800°C (1,346°F–1,472°F)
Hard	745°C–780°C (1,373°F–1,436°F)
Medium	720°C–765°C (1,328°F–1,409°F)
Easy	705°C–725°C (1,301°F–1,337°F)
Extra-easy	665°C–710°C (1,229°F–1,310°F)

157 Soldering surface

This is a surface that you solder onto, made of an asbestos substitute; it is worth having one flat mat and also a few blocks, so that you can create a small hearth to work on.

158 Flux

Flux is a liquid that is used during soldering to keep the metal from oxidizing, so keeping it clean – which is what you need for successful soldering. It also encourages the solder to flow. You paint flux onto the solder seam and the solder. There are two different types of flux that you can use.

Borax

This is the most used and most traditional flux; it comes as a cone, which you dissolve in a dish of water to make a cream-like liquid, which you paint onto the metal. It is very economical, but it can be time-consuming to keep mixing it up.

Auflux

This is a yellow liquid that you buy in a bottle, which is ready to paint on. It is very easy to use.

"AUROFLUX"
Soldering flux for Gold and Silver
Exchange Findings Ltd
49 Hatton Garden, London EC1N 8YS
Tel 0207 400 6500 Fax 0207 400 6577

159 Other soldering materials

• Wire silver solder comes in easy and extra-easy grades and is easier to cut into tiny pieces than the strips.
• Syringe solder comes in a paste form in a syringe, in easy, medium and hard grades. It is very useful when you want tiny amounts of solder.
• Powder solder is used in techniques such as filigree and granulation work.
• Gold solder has a similar grading system but different melting temperatures.
• Tin-based solders are often used for soldering base metals such as copper, brass and so on. Although on some metals you can use silver solder, the advantage of tin solder is that it melts at a lower temperature than silver and is less expensive.

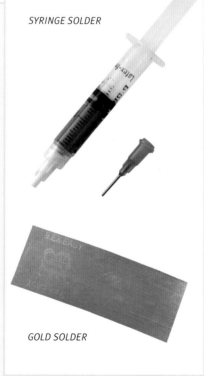

SYRINGE SOLDER

GOLD SOLDER

160 Tweezers

Steel tweezers

These are used for picking up small or hot pieces of metal and also small pieces of solder (known as solder chips or pallions).

Reverse-action tweezers

These are very useful for holding pieces in the right position to be soldered together. You push in on the handles to open the jaws; when released, they clamp shut to hold the piece securely.

Brass or plastic tweezers

These are used for removing soldered items out of the pickle; it is important not to use steel tweezers in the pickle, as this will copperplate the silver with a chemical reaction.

161 Pickling

Once you have soldered a piece, you need an acid – or pickle – to remove the oxides. Safety pickle comes in powder form, to be added to water and heated. Alum also comes in powder form to be added to water and heated, and it is available from pharmacies. Picklean is a new product that comes in powder form, but unlike the others it can be used in cold water, so does not require a pickle pot. You can buy a range of pickle pots, such as a small-scale one for a workshop, or you can use a ceramic slow cooker for this purpose, which is a less expensive option.

162 Polishing equipment

Polishing wheel

A polishing wheel is best used in a permanent workshop set-up, since it creates a lot of mess. It is a motor with detachable mops, usually made of calico or wool. You can also get mops for different finishes.

Drill attachments for polishing

You can buy small polishing and finishing mops for hobby or pendant drills. This is a good low-cost solution for a temporary set-up.

Polish

Polish is what you apply to the mops. Always use separate mops for the different polishes – for example, luster or Tripoli (a brown, waxy block of polish, which is used for the first basic polish) is used on a harder mop and rouge (a red, waxy block of polish for fine finishing) is used on a softer, fluffier one.

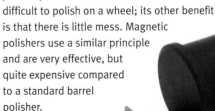

Barrel polisher

This is a revolving drum that contains stainless steel shot, water and a small amount of barrel soap. The drum revolves slowly, burnishing the jewellery inside with the steel shot; it takes about an hour to polish a piece of jewellery. It's ideal for delicate items and chains, which are difficult to polish on a wheel; its other benefit is that there is little mess. Magnetic polishers use a similar principle and are very effective, but quite expensive compared to a standard barrel polisher.

Textured silver pendant

*Add a touch of keum boo to your pieces, using
tip number 264 on page 111.*

CHAPTER FOUR:
Metalwork techniques

This section shows you the most useful techniques and materials to use to start creating professional-looking jewellery designs in metal.

Cutting out

Cutting metal requires only a few basic tools: a saw and a bench pin, or a pair of snips or shears. You do need to practise this technique to perfect it, though. Choosing the correct saw blades and the right tools are key to successful cutting.

You will need a bench pin to saw your metal on, whether this is one that is fixed to a permanent workbench or one that is attached temporarily by a clamp. You can customize your bench pin by cutting out the V-shape required to the angle you like; you can also file out little indents in the end to use for holding bits of metal while filing.

165   **IF YOU DON'T HAVE A BENCH PIN**

FIX IT

You can make your own bench pin out of plywood or scrap wood, about 2.5cm (1in) thick. Cut a 15 x 10cm (6 x 4in) rectangle and then cut a V-shape out of the shorter side. You can then screw a block of wood onto the bottom, about 1 3cm (1 ¼in) from the end, and clamp it onto any table.

163 Choosing a piercing saw blade

Piercing saw blades are very fine and come in different grades, from 0 to 8/0. The higher the number, the finer the blade. Generally you will choose the thickness of your saw blade according to the type of work you are doing – so, for fine, detailed piercing out you would use a high number such as 6/0, whereas for metal thicker than 1mm (18 gauge), you would need a more heavy duty blade such as 1/0 or 2/0. A useful rule is that the metal thickness should be thicker than two of the teeth on the blade.

Assorted piercing saw blades

164 Fastening a saw blade

Learning to put your saw blade in correctly will improve your sawing technique greatly. The important point is to get the blade under tension in the saw frame.

1 Sit at your bench pin, which should be just below chest height. Put your chosen saw frame into the V of your bench pin and rest the handle of the saw frame on your chest; this leaves your hands free.

2 Hold the saw blade with the smooth side of the blade down and the teeth side towards you; make sure you check that the teeth are the right way around (pointing down towards you like the branches of a Christmas tree). Undo the top wing nut on the saw frame and put the blade in, making sure it's the right way around, then tighten the nut, checking that the other end of the blade will align correctly.

3 Undo the bottom nut and let the bottom of the blade drop into the gap. The important thing now is to place your hand on the end of the handle and push forwards on the frame. As you do this, you must tighten the nut without touching the blade, then release it (you will have to push harder than you might think); this puts tension on the blade, which you will need for a good sawing technique.

166 ## Marking out your cut

Marking out what you want to cut out before you begin will help you with precision cutting. There are many ways of transferring a design onto metal; the most traditional way is with a scriber, which scratches a line into the metal. The disadvantages of this are that it is quite tricky to see and it is also difficult to remove if you change your design. Alternatively, you can use a ballpoint or fine permanent pen, which is easier to see and will allow you to alter the line.

If you want to cut a line parallel to the edge of the metal, use dividers. Open them to the width that you want to cut, put one point on the edge of the metal and run the other point down the metal; this produces a straight line. You can only use this method if the edge is perfectly straight on the metal to start with.

Another option is to glue your image onto the metal with water-soluble glue and then cut it out.

167 ## Precision cutting

The most common sawing problems are the result of the blade being too loose or too much force being applied. Expect to break a few blades while you are learning.

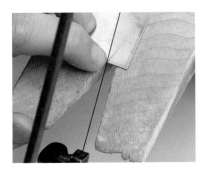

1 Place the piece of metal flat on the bench pin, at the farthest end of the V. Using your left hand as a clamp, hold the metal firmly on the bench pin. It's very important to keep the metal still while you are sawing.

2 Place your saw blade in an upright position, where you want to start sawing. Your sawing hand should be firm, but relaxed. To get the saw started, run the blade upwards on the outside of the line that you want to cut. This gives you the ability to file the line afterwards without making the piece too small. As you start sawing, you can use the edge of your nail to keep the blade in place. Run the saw blade up and down a couple of times to create a small indent, then start sawing up and down.

3 Keep the saw in an upright position – and remember, the downward stroke is the one that is doing the cutting. Try to maintain a steady, rhythmic action, without pushing forwards too much – the blade should do the work. As the cut gets farther along the metal, you may get vibration on the metal, which can jam the blade. To help prevent this, place your index finger from your left hand behind the saw cut to keep the metal still.

TRY IT

168 ### TESTING THE DIRECTION OF THE TEETH

If you find it difficult to see the teeth of the blade, you can feel them by gently running your finger up the blade. It should catch on your skin when you run your fingers up it, and feel smooth when you run them down.

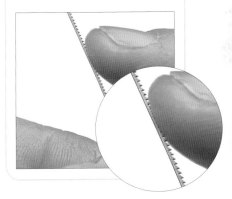

169 ### WHAT TO DO IF YOUR SAW BLADE IS LOOSE

If your blade isn't tight enough when you are sawing, it will be ineffective. Test it by plucking it like a guitar string – it should make a sharp, twanging noise, not a dull, loose noise. If it is too loose, undo the bottom nut and rest the saw frame in the V of the bench pin. Push hard and tighten up the nut again when the saw blade is inside it.

FIX IT

170 Cutting corners

Getting your saw blade to go where you want it to can be a challenge. Turning a corner is a good exercise to help you learn how to guide the saw. The saw blade stays in the same position and the metal moves to follow the line.

Hand-pierced necklace
The magpies and hares on Anna McDade's piece were pierced by hand.

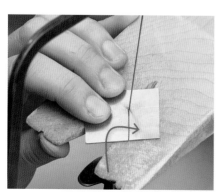

1 Saw forwards along your marked-out line. When you reach the point where you want to turn at a right angle, keep the saw going up and down, without pushing forwards at all, and slowly start turning the piece of metal with your left hand.

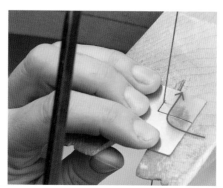

2 The blade should slowly start turning; when you get to the angle that you want, you can recommence sawing normally. You can use a similar technique for following a curve – the saw stays in the same position and the metal is turned.

FIX IT

172 SAW BLADE STICKING?

If you find your blade is sticking in the metal, rub candle wax on it; this can help lubricate it and keep it from sticking.

171 Speedy snips and shears

If you are using thin-gauge metal, you may be able to save time and use snips or shears to cut it, instead of having to use a saw. This can make it easier to cut pieces out, although it is difficult to cut complicated shapes. Snips and shears give a rougher finished edge than a saw blade, since the snips tend to turn up the cutting edge, producing a burr. You will need to file away the burr to ensure that you get a neat edge.

1 Mark out your cutting line. Cut along the outside of the line, so that you have some space to file and refine the shape afterwards.

2 Put the metal you are cutting as far up the jaws of the snips as possible, which will give you a cleaner cut.

3 The turned-up, rough edge produced by the snips needs to be filed to get rid of any burrs created (see page 78).

173 Piercing out a design

Piercing out shapes from metal can create beautifully intricate designs; it involves drilling a hole through which you can pass a saw blade. If you are piercing out very fine details, it is worth using the finest saw blades you can, so that your sawing is more precise. Mark the shapes you want to pierce out carefully, so that there is an easy line to follow.

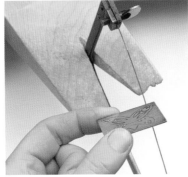

For cutting out shapes, either make your own template or try using stickers or rubber stamps for card making.

1 After marking out the design, use a centre punch and a mallet to make small indentations in the middle of the area to be cut out. Drill a hole (see page 103) large enough to pass a saw blade through.

2 Put the saw blade into the saw frame's top nut, then feed the saw blade through the hole drilled in the metal, with the design side face up. Push the metal up to the top of the frame so that it is not resting on the blade too heavily, then drop the other end of the saw and tighten the bottom nut to create tension on the blade.

Here a sticker, shown in silver, was attached to the metal surface and then used as a template to pierce around.

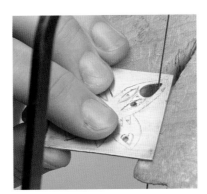

3 You can now pierce out the shapes. It is often easier to cut out all the shapes before cutting the outline, since this leaves you more to hold onto.

TRY IT

174 SAVE THE DUST

If you are cutting out precious metals such as silver or gold, use a bench skin or find some other way of catching the dust produced by sawing. Any metal dust that you collect can be melted down or sold back to a bullion company as scrap, if you have enough. Make sure you don't mix up different metals.

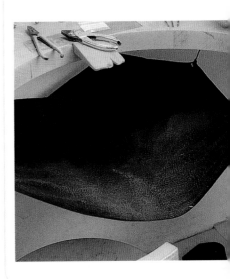

Filing

The purpose of filing is to shape a piece of metal to the outline that you require, and also to remove any marks the saw (or another tool) might have made. There are different profiles, sizes and grades of files to help you achieve a good finish. If you followed the saw line well, the need for filing should be minimal, but filing is a great way to correct any errors from the saw.

"Mobius" ring
Annie Cracknell's ring features numerous soldered seams. Filing each one carefully was critical to achieving a good finish.

175 File profiles

This guide to file profiles will help you to select the correct tool for the piece of jewellery you are making. You can buy needle file sets, which include all of the profiles listed here.

FILE PROFILE	USES
Flat (pillar)	For straight and convex shapes
Half-round	The most useful profile for straight and concave shapes
Triangular	For sharp, V-shaped corners and angles
Square	For right angles
Round	For enlarging holes
Barrette	For sharp corners and making indents for settings
Crossing	For concave shapes

HALF-ROUND   FLAT   CROSSING   BARRETTE

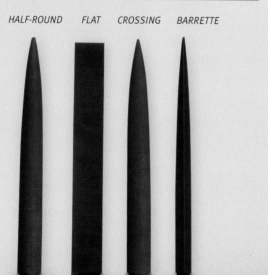

176 Which size and cut?

The length of a file is measured by the cutting surface, not including the end (the tang). Common file sizes are 15cm (6in), or 20cm (8in) for large files, or 10cm (4in) for needle files. There are smaller needle files available for really intricate filing.

Files also come in different cuts, or grades, which determine the amount of metal you can remove:

- **Cut 00** Very coarse, for rapid removal of metal
- **Cut 2** Medium
- **Cut 4** Fine

Most files come without a handle; you can buy the handle separately and attach it yourself, and you can also get detachable handles for needle files.

177 NEED A HANDLE ON YOUR FILE?

To attach a permanent handle to your file, first protect the working face of the file with some fabric. Clamp it into a bench vice with the tang sticking up. Make sure it is secure, then place your wooden handle over the end and tap down on the handle with a mallet until the handle is forced into place.

FIX IT

178 Filing support

Once you have chosen your file profile, size, cut and handle, you can start working on your filing technique. Remember that it is the forward stroke that is cutting the metal away. Files are best used at a 45-degree angle to the metal, which helps keep the file from digging into the metal and creating ridges.

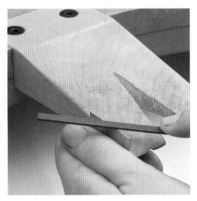

1 It is a good idea to support the piece of metal that you are filing, either by holding it up against the bench pin or, especially if it is something quite small, putting it in a ring clamp or vice.

2 The easiest way to hold a file is to put it in the palm of your hand and put the index finger of your other hand on the top of the file. This allows you to apply downward pressure while you are filing. When you have finished filing with one grade of file, you can use a finer one to get a better finish, before finally sanding the piece (see page 105).

TRY IT

180 GETTING IT STRAIGHT

If you're finding that your straight edges are not perfect, there are ways to get things back on track.

1 When you are trying to file a straight line, often a natural action is to drop the file off at the end of the metal. However, this will result in a slight curve at the end of the metal.

2 To prevent this curving, try to keep your file parallel to the metal

179 Filing seams

Use a half-round needle file to refine the seam on the inside of a ring or any concave shape. It will make the seam invisible, once it is filed and sanded (see page 105).

1 Place the file to the left of the solder seam, with the right-hand side of it tipped downwards.

2 Pass the file through the ring over the seam, gradually turning it so that the stroke is finished on the right-hand side of the seam, with the left-hand side of the file tipping down. Repeat this action. Turn the ring around and file the other side in the same way.

181 Riffler files

Because of their turned-up shape, riffler files are useful for getting into hard-to-reach places that a straight file would fail to get to. They are usually double ended, with a different profile at each end.

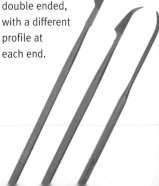

182 Filing sheet metal for bending

This is a useful technique for creating right angles in metal – for example, when making a box. The key to success is marking out accurately and scoring neatly, because if the angle of the line is not scored at a right angle to the bottom of the metal, it will make the bend lopsided.

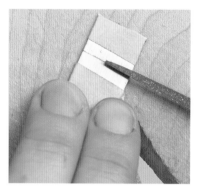

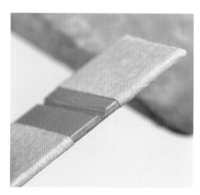

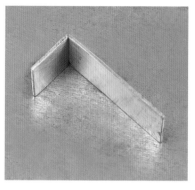

1 Score a line at a right angle to the base of the metal where you want to bend the metal. Protect the metal with masking tape, leaving the scored line exposed. Place a triangular file on the scored line and file.

2 Stop filing when you are just over halfway through the thickness of the metal and have created a V-shaped ridge.

3 Put the sheet of metal on a steel block with the fold line over the edge, and tap down with a mallet until you have a 90-degree angle.

183 Removing filing burrs

A burr is a build-up of metal that occurs when filing, which creates a sharp overhang on the edge of the metal. Burrs need to be removed by filing.

1 Over the course of filing the metal edge, a burr has been created and needs to be removed.

2 Take your file and run it backwards at an angle along the outer edge of your metal piece; this will pull the burr off the edge of the metal.

184 WHAT TO DO IF YOUR FILE ISN'T WORKING

Over time, files will clog up with metal dust, making them ineffective. Clean them by regularly brushing them with a file brush or a soft brass bristle brush. Rubbing chalk onto the cutting surface will also help to prevent a file from clogging.

FIX IT

185 Finding the right file

Different-shaped files are appropriate for different applications, sizes of pieces and level of finish you require. The file you choose will also depend on whether you are filing the inside or the outside of a curved piece, for example.

Pierced curves For a pierced-out piece with an edge that curves in and out, you will need both a small flat file and an oval or half-round one. The edge will have marks left by the saw, which can be removed by filing.

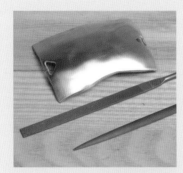

Angled edges To file an angled edge, hold a flat file at an angle of 45 degrees against the edge of the piece and use a smooth, forward stroke to make a neat edge.

Inside curves On the curve that goes into the work, use an oval or half-round file, with the same action as for the inside curve of a ring (see page 77).

Inside bends Use a triangular file to get into small areas that need filing and to help create a bend in wire or sheet metal. File a groove just over halfway through the metal, then bend it carefully upwards, so that it forms a right angle.

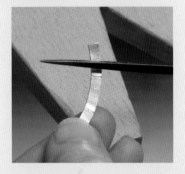

Outside curves For the outer curve, use a small flat file with a straight-over action until it cannot reach the next inner curve.

Right angles Use a square file to file a right angle. You can also use it in the same way as the triangular file to make the groove for bending a right angle.

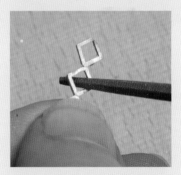

Circle edges To file the edge of a pierced-out circle, always use a flat file and work down to the scribed line.

Grooves and holes Use a round file to file a curved groove for tubing or to help open out a round hole. When filing in a hole, be careful not to file an unintentional groove.

Joining metal

There are several ways of joining different pieces and types of metal together, including soldering, fusing, hinging, riveting and bolting.

Your choice of metal and design will dictate which form of joining you will need to use. Whichever method you decide on, you can disguise it or make a feature of it, depending on the look you want to achieve.

HEALTH AND SAFETY

Follow these simple safety steps:
- Tie up your hair
- Remove scarves
- Keep a fire extinguisher, fire blanket and first-aid kit near your workbench

186 What is silver soldering?

Soldering is a method of joining two or more pieces of metal together by melting solder (a metal alloy) into the seam between the two metals. The most common type of solder in jewellery making is silver solder. It will take a little practice to be confident at soldering; it is worth trying with a base metal first, such as brass or copper.

Silver soldering tools and materials:

- Torch
- Heatproof soldering block
- Silver solder
- Flux
- Paintbrush
- Steel tweezers
- Brass tweezers
- Pickle and container
- Snips

188 Five rules of soldering

To achieve good soldering results the metals being soldered must have a very tight seam, with no gaps; the metal also needs to be clean before you start. The next important step is to paint the pieces of metal to be soldered with flux. Flux keeps the metal from oxidizing – it keeps the metal clean – while it is being heated. The flux only needs to be applied to the areas to be soldered.

1 Make a tight seam.
2 Flux the metal and solder.
3 Heat the two pieces evenly.
4 Heat the metal, not the solder.
5 Start with the highest temperature solder and go down to the lowest temperature one.

TRY IT

187 USING THE CORRECT PART OF THE FLAME

Light your torch and look at the flame (it's easier to look at it in dim lighting). You will see that there is a bluer area, and just in front of this is the hottest part of the flame: this is where you want to heat the metal. The blue part itself is where there is more oxygen, and it is known as an oxidizing flame. This area is cooler. Experiment with heating the metal. You will find that if you bring the torch in too close, the metal actually gets cooler and the torch starts making a louder roaring noise (if you hear this, you are holding the torch too close).

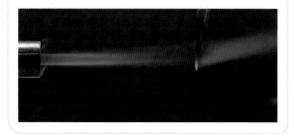

189 Mixing borax

You buy borax in the form of a cone that comes with a shallow flat dish that you dissolve it in. To make the flux, dip the cone in some water and put it into the dish. Grind it around, as if using a mortar and pestle, and keep dipping it into the water until you get a cream-like consistency in the dish. This is now ready to use as a flux, which you paint on with a paintbrush. Because the dish is porous, the watery flux dries up quickly, which means you have to mix it up each time you want to solder.

190 Which grade of solder?

Start with the highest-temperature solder and move down the grades. The names are an indication of the melting temperature and not how strong the solder is.

When you are soldering something that you will need to solder more than once, such as the ring on page 82, it is important that you use the correct grade of solder. This is because when you silver solder, you have to heat the metal and not the solder. If you use the same grade of solder to solder the wire onto the metal as to solder the ring seam at the back, you risk the wires at the front moving or falling off while you are soldering the seam at the back, because the solder would flow at the same temperature. What you need to do is drop down a temperature grade of solder: use medium solder to solder the wires on, then use easy solder for the seam at the back of the ring. It is always worth leaving yourself the chance to use extra-easy solder in case you need to repair or adjust anything at the end.

SOLDER NAME	MELTING TEMPERATURE
Enamelling	730°C–800°C (1,346°F–1,472°F)
Hard	745°C–780°C (1,373°F–1,436°F)
Medium	720°C–765°C (1,328°F–1,409°F)
Easy	705°C–725°C (1,301°F–1,337°F)
Extra-easy	665°C–710°C (1,229°F–1,310°F)

HARD   MEDIUM   EASY   EXTRA-EASY

191 Where to apply heat?

Solder will only flow and join the pieces together when the metal gets to the temperature that the solder melts at, so you must heat the metal near the solder, not just the solder. The solder will 'jump' onto the piece of metal that gets hottest, so it is important, when you are soldering a small piece of metal onto a larger piece of metal, not to overheat the small piece (as the solder will jump onto it). You need to concentrate more heat on the larger piece so that both pieces of metal reach the same temperature at the same time, allowing the solder to flow and join the two pieces together. Silver solder flows by capillary action when the metal is hot. If done well, a solder seam should be as strong as the metal.

192 Preventing and removing firestain

What is it? Firestain shows as grey or purple shadowy marks on polished sterling silver and low-karat gold, which prevents a highly reflective surface. It shows mainly on larger pieces of flat silver. Try putting your polished object on a piece of white paper: if you have firestain you'll see grey marks on the surface.

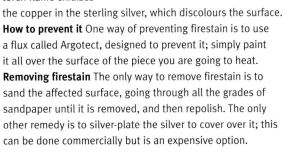

The reason it happens The oxygen in the air and in the torch flame oxidizes the copper in the sterling silver, which discolours the surface.

How to prevent it One way of preventing firestain is to use a flux called Argotect, designed to prevent it; simply paint it all over the surface of the piece you are going to heat.

Removing firestain The only way to remove firestain is to sand the affected surface, going through all the grades of sandpaper until it is removed, and then repolish. The only other remedy is to silver-plate the silver to cover over it; this can be done commercially but is an expensive option.

193 Soldering wire decorations

This soldering technique applies to all types of silver soldering, whether it is for adding metal embellishments, as here, or soldering seams.

Silver soldered ring
This simple silver ring has been embellished with soldered gold wire.

1 Cut and shape the wire to be soldered, making sure that it fits the piece of metal you are going to solder it onto (in this case, completely flat). You can flatten it on a steel block with a mallet to get both the wire and metal flat. Paint flux (borax or Auflux) onto the area of the metal to be soldered and the bottom of the wire to be soldered.

2 Place the wire in position. Cut some small pieces of solder (pallions) with snips, one for each end of the wire. The grade of solder you use will depend on how many times you need to solder to complete your design. In this example, medium solder is used to solder on the wire and easy solder is used to solder up the seam of the ring.

3 Dip the pieces of solder into the flux and, using steel tweezers, place them at the ends of the wire. It is better to use as small a piece of solder as you can, because if the piece is too big, it will leave behind blobs of excess solder, which can be hard to remove.

FIX IT

194 FILLING GAPS IN YOUR SOLDER SEAM

You can fill any imperfections with solder. The important thing is to use a lower temperature grade of solder than you have used before, so you don't risk the last bit of soldering running again. Flux the area to be filled, cut some reasonably large pieces of solder, flux them, and place them over the imperfection. Heat the whole piece of metal until the solder just flows, then quickly remove the flame. Pickle the piece. You can now remove the excess solder with a file to see if it has filled the imperfection; if it has not, just repeat the process.

4 Light your torch. Use a low flame to start with and begin to gently heat the whole piece of metal. Often the flux can bubble and move the pieces of wire and solder, so you may need to reposition them. Turn the torch up a little and continue evenly heating the piece of metal. When both pieces reach the same temperature that the solder melts at, the solder will flow along the seam between the two pieces of metal. You will need to watch closely and, once you see this happen, remove the flame; you may see a white line of solder run along the wire.

5 Pick up the metal with steel tweezers and quench it in water, then place it in the warm pickle pot. Leave it for about five minutes or until the oxide is removed and it is clean – which, in the case of silver, means matte white. Remove it from the pickle with brass tweezers – never the steel ones, because if you put steel tweezers into the pickle they will cause the pickle to copper-plate any silver in it, by electrolytic action. Rinse the metal with water to wash away the pickle.

195 Soldering sheets of metal

When soldering one metal sheet to another, the same principles as soldering wire apply, with slight differences. This method will ensure a neat and more professional finish. This example shows a copper heart being soldered onto a silver pendant.

1 Take the heart and paint flux onto the back of it, then cut a couple of pieces of medium solder, dip them in the flux and place them on the back of the heart. The number of pieces will depend on the size of the piece.

2 Light the torch and heat the heart until the solder runs over the back of it, then quench in water and pickle it for five minutes. Once clean, remove it from the pickle using brass tweezers and rinse with water.

3 Flux the back of the heart again (which has the solder pre-melted onto it) and add flux to the piece of metal it's being soldered to. Place it where you want it.

4 Reheat the whole piece until the solder reflows and solders the two pieces together. It is a little more difficult to see when the solder flows. Look out for a whiter shiny line appearing at the edge of the metal: once this has happened, remove the torch, quench and pickle again.

197 WHY DIDN'T IT SOLDER?

FIX IT

These are the most common reasons why pieces do not join successfully:

- The seam wasn't good enough
- The metal wasn't clean
- The metal wasn't fluxed
- The metal didn't get hot enough
- One piece of metal got hotter than the other
- There was pickle left on the metal before soldering

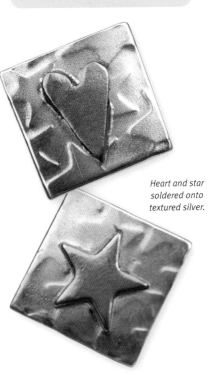

Heart and star soldered onto textured silver.

196 Using syringe solder

Syringe solder comes in different grades (hard, medium and easy) in paste form inside a syringe. To use the syringe you squeeze the plunger, which dispenses small amounts of solder paste. The paste is pre-fluxed, but this doesn't mean that you don't need flux on the metal (a common mistake); it means that the solder has flux within the paste. Syringe solder is especially useful when you need tiny amounts of solder. It sticks to the metal, so it is particularly good for seams on which it would be awkward to balance pieces of strip solder, such as chain links. It also means no more cutting tiny pieces of solder, which saves a lot of time.

It is generally not used for soldering larger objects, because the flux within the solder paste is often used up before the piece has heated enough for the solder to run, which turns it crumbly and grey.

198 Fusing principles

Fusing is a way of joining metal with heat but without the use of solder. It is mainly suitable for silver or gold, because the temperatures required for fusing base metals are too high for basic torches. The principle is that the surfaces to be fused will join at the temperature at which the metal starts to melt; each surface slightly melts and exchanges material with the other surface, creating a bond. It can be a hard process to control and is often difficult to repeat.

Fused decorations
These silver rings are embellished with fused gold balls.

199 Fusing wire

Fusing can produce a textured, organic surface that will enhance your jewellery pieces.

1 Wrap pieces of silver wire together as you want them to fuse. Place them on the heat-proof block and start to heat them. Because the wire is thin, you must be careful not to heat any one area too much, since the wire will melt. Keep the flame moving so that it all heats up to the temperature at which silver melts (approximately 893°C/1,640°F), when it will be a bright red. You will see the wires start to melt together. You can do it enough so that the pieces just bond, or you can leave it longer until the pieces join together.

2 Finish the piece off by pickling it, then wash and dry it.

Bird in a nest pendant
This pendant uses fused wire to represent a nest for the golden bird soldered to it.

200 Making fused balls for decoration

You can melt small pieces of silver, gold, brass or copper into balls – although the brass and copper will need to be at a very high temperature, so you will only be able to make small balls. These balls can then be soldered onto a piece as decoration.

If you want to make balls of a uniform size, cut pieces of wire of the same length. If you want completely round balls, make round indentations in the charcoal block first. If you want to solder the balls onto a flat surface, it can be easier to have a slightly flat bottom – in this case, melt them on a flat heat-proof mat (1). To make a ball, heat needs to be applied; light the torch and aim it directly at the piece of wire (2). Quite quickly it will go bright red and shrink into a ball (3). When it is completely molten, it will begin to spin. Once this happens, remove the flame and pickle the ball.

201 Guidelines for pewter soldering

It is possible to solder pewter using a soft tin solder and liquid flux. You can use a torch, but the main difference is that you are not heating the pewter – instead, you are heating the solder. This is because pewter has a very low melting point, so you must take the torch away as soon as the solder melts to avoid melting your piece. It is a good idea to practise this first on a piece that isn't too important.

203 Joining without heat

You can join metals together without using heat by riveting. Some metals, such as aluminium and titanium, can only be riveted because they can't be soldered, but you can use this technique with any metal. It is also handy for incorporating materials such as wood or acrylic, which cannot be heated. There are three types of rivets: tube, wire and stilt.

204 Wire riveting

Wire riveting is a fairly simple technique; it's all about getting your measurements correct. You can either make the rivets so that they are flush to the surface of the metal and seem to disappear, or they can be slightly raised to become a feature. You can also use a different-coloured metal rivet from the metal pieces it's joining, which can be an attractive feature.

202 Gold soldering

The principles of gold soldering are the same as for silver soldering – you heat the metal rather than the solder. Nine-karat gold solder reacts slightly differently – it doesn't flow as easily as silver – whereas 18-karat gold reacts very similarly to silver solder. The melting temperatures of gold solder are different to those of silver, and different-coloured gold solders – yellow, red, or white – are also available.

9 karat yellow	Hard 725°C (1,337°F)
	Medium 735°C (1,355°F)
	Easy 650°C (1,202°F)
	Extra-easy 620°C (1,148°F)
9 karat white	725°C (1,337°F)
9 karat red	735°C (1,355°F)
18 karat yellow	Hard 790°C (1,454°F)
	Medium 730°C (1,346°F)
	Easy 700°C (1,292°F)
18 karat red	805°C (1,481°F)
18 karat white	Hard 855°C (1,571°F)
	Medium 705°C (1,301°F)
	Easy 690°C (1,274°F)
14 karat yellow	Medium 721°C (1,330°F)

205 Riveting layers

Riveting is useful for pieces where you want to include materials that can't be soldered, such as acrylic. For this technique, cut the two pieces of brass and a sheet of coloured acrylic and polish them (see pages 106–108) before beginning. On the top layer of brass, measure and mark out where you want the rivets to go and, with a centre punch and a mallet, make a small indentation where you are going to drill a hole. This is so the drill will locate.

1 Tape the three pieces together and clamp them, so they can't move. Choose a drill bit the same size as the wire that you are using as a rivet – in this case, 1.2mm (16 gauge). Drill through all three pieces, in all the places you want the rivets, then neaten up the holes. Remove the tape.

2 Measure the depth of all three pieces while sandwiched together and cut a piece of wire 1mm ($^1/_{32}$in) longer than this depth. File both ends flat and push the rivet into one of the holes.

3 Place all three pieces on a steel block and use the riveting hammer to tap on the end of the wire that you have just filed until it splays the metal out, then turn it over and tap again on the other side. Now the rivet should be nice and tight. Repeat for the other three rivets.

TRY IT

206 CONCEALED RIVETING

To conceal your rivets and make them flush with the surface of the metal, you need to countersink the holes for them. Use a slightly larger drill bit than you need for drilling the hole (if the hole is 1mm/$^{1}/_{32}$in, use a 1.5mm/$^{1}/_{16}$in drill bit and drill a little way into the metal). This will give you a cone-shaped indentation. Make and fit the rivet (see page 85). Instead of standing proud of the metal, the rivet will fit into the indentation, making it almost invisible if done in the same metal.

207 Tube riveting

A tube rivet works on the same principle as the wire rivet. It can be useful if you want to retain a hole through a piece for fittings, such as ear wires.

1 Measure and mark where you want the rivet on the two pieces of metal you are going to join. Centre punch an indentation and drill a hole the same size as the outside diameter of the tubing.

2 Cut a piece of tubing approximately 1mm ($^{1}/_{32}$in) longer than the depth of the two pieces of metal, then file and sand the ends.

3 Put the pieces of metal on a steel block, put the piece of tubing in the hole and place a centre punch inside the tubing. Tap it with a mallet to splay out the edges of the tubing.

4 Turn the piece over and do the same to the other end of the tubing. Now the two pieces should be secured.

5 Take a flat steel hammer or a punch and flatten down the end of the tube on the sheet metal.

208 Stilt riveting

A stilt rivet is useful if you want to join two pieces of metal together but retain a gap between them. You will need a piece of wire that is the same diameter as the inside diameter of the tubing.

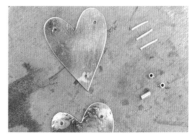

1 Measure and mark where you want the rivets to be and drill the holes through the two pieces of metal to be riveted. The holes need to be the same diameter as the wire that you are using.

2 Measure the distance you want to create between the two pieces of metal, then saw the pieces of tubing to this length. Now cut the pieces of wire that will pass through the tubing. They need to be 1mm ($^{1}/_{32}$in) longer than the tubing and the thickness of the two pieces of metal. Assemble all the pieces like a sandwich. The tubing fits over the wire in the middle of the sandwich, holding the two pieces of metal apart.

3 Now use a riveting hammer to finish the rivets.

Making the perfect hinge

Hinges are useful where you want to have movement between two pieces, such as the lid of a box, or in a locket or bangle. Hinges are constructed using rivets. The keys to making a successful hinge are getting the measurements of the materials correct and the accuracy of the soldering. This sequence will give you an example of how to make a simple hinged pendant; there are other variations of hinges that are used in different situations.

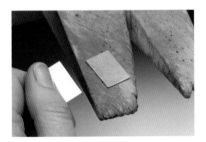

1 Saw out two pieces of 0.8-mm (22-gauge) metal the same size. If you are doing any soldering at this stage, use a hard solder.

2 Cut a piece of the tubing the same length as one side of the sheet metal, file the ends and solder it to the edge of the metal, using a lower-temperature solder (medium) than has been used anywhere on the pieces of metal. Pickle and wash the piece.

3 Measure and mark this piece of tubing into three even pieces (for a long hinge you may need five pieces).

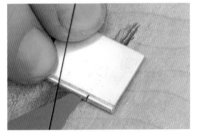

4 Using a saw, cut straight down at right angles, through the lines you have marked, down to the sheet metal.

5 Then cut across into the corners. The aim is to remove the central piece of tubing.

6 File out the remaining bit of tubing until it is removed completely, so that the remaining two pieces of tubing are totally in line with each other.

7 Measure the gap between the two pieces of tubing and cut another piece of tube that fits into the gap. Place the two pieces of metal to be hinged alongside each other and mark where the small piece of tubing is to be soldered. Solder the tubing on, with medium solder. Pickle and wash. Put the two pieces together to check that they line up. Polish the two pieces (see pages 106–108).

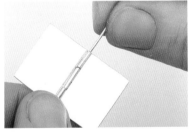

8 Measure the length of the whole hinge and cut a piece of wire of the same diameter as the inside diameter of the tubing, adding on 1mm ($\frac{1}{32}$in) to the length. Push the wire into the end of the tubing; it needs to be a tight fit to be able to rivet successfully. Feed it through all three pieces of tubing until approximately 1.5mm ($\frac{1}{16}$in) is poking out of either end.

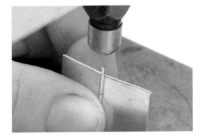

9 Put the hinge upright on a steel block and, using a riveting hammer, tap the end of the wire. Turn the piece around and do the same to the other end. Do this a couple of times to force the end of the wire to splay out, keeping it from coming back out of the tubing.

Texturing metal

Texturing metal is a great way of adding decorative interest to your jewellery. There are many different techniques to try.

You can apply texture at different stages in the making of a piece of jewellery. It is frequently done pre-assembly and often can't be added after the assembly is complete, so it is crucial to factor it into the design of your piece. Having an interesting texture can transform a fairly ordinary design into one in which the texture becomes the focal point.

HEALTH AND SAFETY
Gravers are extremely sharp. You should always try to work away from yourself, rather than turning the graver towards you. It is very easy to slip, so care needs to be taken.

210 Engraving

Engraving is the technique of scraping away metal to create surface lines and decoration; it requires some specialist tools and a steady hand. It is important to hold the piece of metal to be engraved firmly – you can use an engraver's vice, or alternatively, you could embed your piece of metal into pitch, which is a tar-like substance. If you are engraving by hand, you will need gravers to cut lines in the metal; the most useful profiles are square-ended, lozenge, chisel-ended, and spit stick, which is also used for removing metal from settings for stones.

If you prefer not to engrave by hand, you can use a pendant drill. This electric tool has different burrs and diamond-tipped tools to create all kinds of different effects.

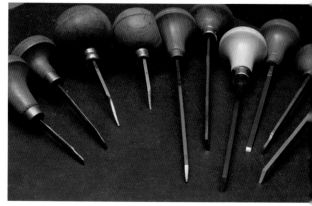

Hand engravers
A selection of gravers with different-shaped ends for achieving various decorative effects.

211 Adding a simple hand-engraved design

This simple design uses only straight lines. Make sure that your graver is sharp, no matter what pattern you are attempting (to sharpen it, use a sharpening stone with a little oil).

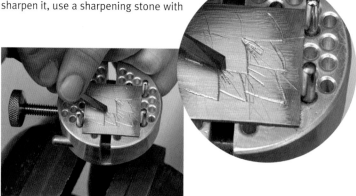

1 Place the handle of your engraver's vice into a bench vice or embed it in pitch. Mark out your design, using a steel rule, with a scriber or pen. Then place the metal to be engraved securely into the engraver's vice.

2 Use a lozenge-shaped graver, keep it vertical, then bring it down, so that the graver digs into the metal. Hold it at an angle of less than 45 degrees. Put your index finger on top of the graver and apply downward pressure. Push forwards slowly, cutting away from yourself in small strokes. Make all the lines going in one direction first; you can deepen them by using a different-shaped graver. Turn the engraver's vice around to engrave the other lines.

212 Engraved effects

Whether engraving by hand or using a pendant drill, you will be able to achieve an enormous variety of engraved finishes on different substrates.

Substrate: Brass 1–2

1 A circle was marked with a scribe and the interior engraved with a small round cutting tool, the 'frazier' on a pendant drill. Outer lines were made with a tapered diamond burr.
2 Effect achieved using a silicone rubber wheel on a pendant drill.

Substrate: Silver 3–5

3 Sketched with a scribe and engraved with a lozenge hand graver. It was oxidized and the surface cleaned with fine wet-and-dry paper.
4 Flower pattern sketched with a soft pencil and engraved with a lozenge graver.
5 Triangles marked using a template and scribe. The top triangle was marked with a round-edge graver, the centre triangle with a lozenge graver and the lowest triangle with a knife-edge graver.

Substrate: Copper 6–7

6 Sketchy engraving done with a tapered diamond burr applied in different directions. The burr was held in a pendant drill.
7 Pattern outlined with a scribe and engraved using a parallel diamond burr and a small round-headed diamond burr.

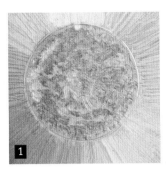

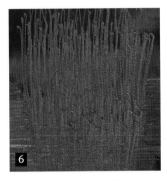
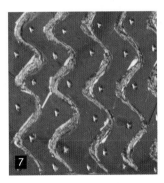

213 A GRAVE ERROR

If you slip with the graver, as long as it's not too deep a gouge, you can try to burnish it out (see Removing scratches, page 106). If it is a bad gouge on a silver piece, you could run some silver solder into the area to fill it and then sand it flush again.

FIX IT

214 Using a pendant drill

There are various types of workbench-based pendant drills to which different burrs and cutters can be fitted. Diamond burrs are supplied either as a cone, disc, round or parallel-shaped, and are sharp enough to give a good cut into areas required. 'Ball-shaped' cutters in fine, medium and coarse grades make a round, hollowing cut. Less aggressive burrs will simply mark smooth linear patterns or crosshatching.

The pendant drill is also an excellent tool for cleaning and polishing small areas. Wet-and-dry paper can be fixed into a split spindle to smooth the inner side of rings. Fine silicon rubber points, in a variety of shapes, will give a clean satin finish to metal, and there are others made especially to give a great shine on platinum. Small felt brushes and mops are used with the same polishes as are used on large polishing motors.

215 Planishing

This is a fairly easy technique, which will make your piece of jewellery look handcrafted. It was a technique used in the Arts and Crafts period of the late nineteenth and early twentieth centuries. To create an overall planished pattern, use a round-ended steel hammer, such as a repoussé or ball peen hammer. If you are making a ring with a planished finish, you will need to planish the ring band first and then cut the ring size to length, since the planishing will lengthen the piece of metal.

1 Put the piece of metal on a steel block and, using a round-ended hammer, hit the metal. This will create an indentation. Try to contact the metal at a 45-degree angle.

2 Repeat the hammering with a rhythmic action, trying to slightly overlap the last indentation and being careful not to hit too hard on the edges, which can get distorted.

216 Hammered textures

By using different-shaped hammers, you can create different textures. Shown here are some examples next to the hammers or tools that created them. You can also buy metal stamps with indented designs on the ends, such as lettering, numbers and little patterns. To use these, simply place them where you want the design to be and hit the end with a mallet.

1 Planishing hammer edge
2 Round-ended planishing hammer edge
3 Riveting hammer end
4 Raising hammer
5 Ball peen hammer
6 Large round-ended hammer
7 Letter and number stamps
8 Repoussé hammer
9 Planishing hammer edge

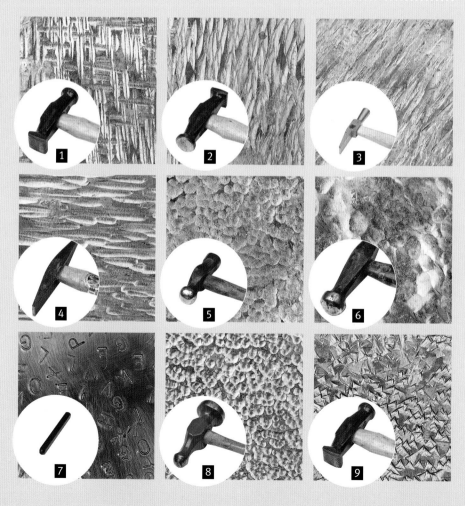

Using a rolling mill effectively

A great way of adding texture and pattern is by using a rolling mill. It is amazing what objects and textures will make indentations in metal, including feathers, skeleton leaves and fabric. It's worth trying objects out first with scrap metal to see if they make a successful pattern. You can also buy pre-made brass texture plates. The key to making a good impression is getting the depth on the rolling mill correct for the thickness of metal you are using. Again, test the depth using a piece of scrap metal, ensuring it is the same thickness as the metal of your piece. Never put steel wire or textures through the mill, because they will damage the rollers. Anneal (see page 94) the piece of metal before you put it through the mill; this softens it, allowing it to take the impression better. Pickle and wash it and make sure it is dry before it goes through the rollers.

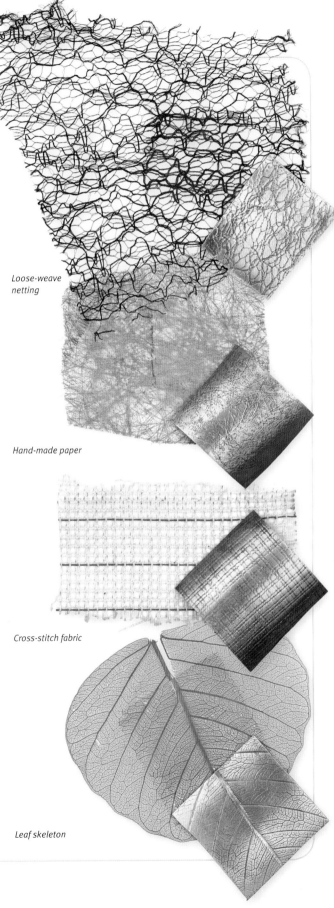

Loose-weave netting

Hand-made paper

Cross-stitch fabric

Leaf skeleton

1 Place your chosen texture, in this case a piece of mesh fabric, on top of the metal and against the rollers, then start to turn the handle away from you and feed the metal through. As the metal comes out the other side, you will see the texture on the metal.

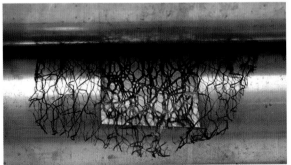

2 It is always best to texture the piece of metal before cutting, because the pressure from the rolling mill can distort the edges. As it comes out the other side of the mill it distorts and curls up, so you will need to flatten the metal down again with a mallet. Now you can pierce out your design.

218 Inlaying coloured wires using a rolling mill

The effect of this technique makes it look as if the wires have been inlaid into the metal sheet; you could then put a texture over the whole piece, to create an interesting surface effect.

Copper wire was rolled flush to the surface with a fabric texture added over the top.

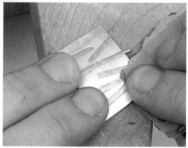

1 Shape the wires to your chosen design and solder them onto the metal sheet. The wires need to be around half the thickness of the metal you are using. They must be well-soldered onto the surface, since they will be under a huge amount of pressure in the rolling mill and may come loose.

2 Once the wires are soldered, pickle, wash and dry the piece. Adjust the roller depth until they are slightly narrower than the thickness of the wire height, then feed the metal through the rollers; this will slightly compress the wires. Adjust the rollers, a little narrower, and roll again. Keep doing this until the wires are flush with the surface.

3 The wires will appear to be wider than when they started, because they have been compressed and flattened during rolling. Sand over the surface to get a good finish, then cut out your design.

Examples of copper etching, using stickers as a resist.

219 Etching resists

Etching is a way of putting a relief pattern onto metal, using a resist and a chemical. Traditionally, the chemicals used for etching are acids: sulphuric acid for copper-based metals and nitric acid for silver. These are highly dangerous to handle and are not suitable for a temporary workshop set-up. There are safer chemicals that you can use and the technique remains the same.

Safe etching chemicals include ferric chloride, which is used for copper-based metals such as brass, bronze, copper and nickel silver (not sterling silver). Ferric nitrate is used for silver. These chemicals are salts rather than acids, which makes them easier to buy and safer to use.

To etch on metal you need a resist to the chemicals, meaning a material that can be put on the surface that will remain untouched by them.

RESIST MATERIAL	TECHNIQUE
Stop-out varnish	Painted on with a brush over the whole surface of the metal and then scratched off.
Permanent pens	Ordinary permanent oil-based markers or fineline pens that are drawn onto the metal.
Pre-cut sticky labels	Including stickers used for card making, lettering and shapes.
Tape	Masking tape or sticky tape from which you cut out a design to stick on the metal.

220 Etching with pen and sticker resists

This method is shown on copper; it can also be used on silver, but use ferric nitrate as the etching chemical instead.

1 Clean the piece of metal to be etched with an abrasive cleaner and create your resist design; here, pre-cut stickers and permanent pens were used. It's important to cover up the whole back area of the metal and the edges, including inside any holes; you can do this with permanent pen or sticky tape.

2 Put on rubber gloves and prepare the ferric chloride in a plastic container according to the manufacturer's instructions. This chemical works best if it is warmed a little, so if you think you will want to do a lot of etching, it may be worth buying a dedicated slow cooker for it. Ideally, the metal needs to be suspended in the solution upside down – you can hang the metal on a piece of wire – but you can just put it into the solution face up and it will still work perfectly well. Leave it for up to two hours. Keep checking every half hour, to see if the etch is as deep as you want. A weak solution will take longer.

3 When you are happy with the result, remove it from the bath using plastic tweezers and rinse it. Be careful where the solution drips, since it leaves a bright yellow stain. Scrub the surface of the metal with baking soda, which neutralizes the chemical and stops the etching. Remove the resist with white spirit and polish the surface.

TRY IT

221 RUBBER STAMPS

For a really unique, detailed pattern or texture, you can use rubber stamps of the kind used in card making. Stamp your rubber stamp using a permanent ink pad or draw with permanent pens over the surface of the stamp and print it onto the metal. This can create an interesting, detailed image.

222 Rippling with reticulation

Reticulation is a surface texture that is achieved with heat. It creates a wrinkled, rippled effect on the surface of silver; it can also be done on gold, but not on base metals. It creates an interesting organic background texture for jewellery.

For reticulation to work well, you need to create a top layer of fine silver (on sterling silver). You can achieve this by annealing (see page 94) and pickling the piece of sterling silver six or seven times; this brings the copper in the sterling silver to the surface, which is then pickled away, leaving a fine silver surface behind.

1 Put your annealed piece of silver on a charcoal or heat-proof block. Light your torch and heat the silver until it becomes a deep red, then start to move and concentrate the flame, making areas become bright red. The surface will start to shimmer and become molten. Move the torch around the whole piece of silver until you have created the effect all over. Be careful not to overheat areas, since you may melt holes in the silver. Continue until you are pleased with the effect, then pickle and wash the piece. Now you can continue with your design.

2 Polish the piece to a satin finish with a wire brush: this is the best way to finish reticulated jewellery. If it is highly polished, it can lose definition.

Reticulated wrap-over ring with a topaz set in a tapered collet.

Shaping metal

Shaping metal adds a three-dimensional element to jewellery, creating effects that enhance its reflective qualities. Using the right tools for the job is key to getting a good finish and the right profile.

This fine silver pendant has been heavily shaped and folded.

If you are forging or shaping a piece of metal, you first need to anneal it. You will also need to anneal it again every time it starts to work-harden. (When you shape metal, particularly with steel hammers, you will find that the metal becomes very tough and unmalleable and can also become brittle.) Annealing the metal means heating it up until it becomes a dull red colour, then quenching in water and pickling it (see page 69). This will make the metal more malleable, so you can continue to work on it.

Annealing realigns the metal's molecular structure, making all its molecules face in the same direction; this is what makes the metal easier to bend.

When you hammer the metal, this disturbs its molecules, making them go in different directions, which has the effect of toughening the metal. Silver, copper and brass don't need to stay hot to be malleable. Even when the metal is quenched or cooled, it retains its malleability, unlike ferrous metals such as steel, which harden when quenched.

223 Annealing metal in five easy steps

Most sheet silver you can buy has been pre-annealed, so it won't need annealing when you first start to work on it.

1 To begin annealing, place the metal on the soldering block; there is no need to flux it.

2 Light the torch and heat up the whole piece of metal until it becomes a dullish red colour.

3 Try not to overheat areas so they glow bright red, since this can also make the metal brittle.

4 Quench the metal in water and then place in the pickle for five minutes or until clean.

5 Then rinse and it is ready to use.

224 Bending or forging?

Both bending and forging alter the shape of metal, the difference being that when you bend metal the thickness stays the same, whereas with forging you are changing the thickness and profile of the metal. Generally, for shaping and bending metal you would use a mallet and for forging you would use steel hammers.

To bend metal, you need a shape or former to bend the metal against, as well as pliers, formers and mandrels. It is important to have the correct formers for the shape you want to make. When you are using metal hammers and formers it is important to keep them in good condition, because any mark on the hammer or the former will transfer onto the metal, which can be difficult to remove.

TRY IT

225 ANNEALING WIRE
Thin wire can be difficult to anneal without overheating areas. Also, if it's a large amount of wire, it can be difficult to fit it on a soldering block. Try winding it into a coil, with the ends tucked in, and gently heat it all over. This will reduce the risk of melting the wire.

226 Basic metal shaping

Flattening sheet: If you want to flatten a piece of sheet metal that has been curved, place it on a steel block so that the piece is convex and there is a gap between the steel block and the metal. Then, using a mallet, tap it flat with a downward motion.

Bending wire: You can bend wire with pliers, and for thicker wire, you can use mandrels. Round wire (shown here) is the easiest to bend in any direction, while square, oval or other profiles will only easily bend one way without their profiles becoming distorted.

FIX IT

228 KINKY WIRE?

Wire can be difficult to straighten once it has kinks in it, but here's a trick to try. Put one end of the wire into the jaws of a bench vice and hold the other end with a pair of flat pliers. Start to twist the wire in one direction – just a few turns, not too many or the wire may break. As well as straightening out the wire, this also strengthens it. Another way of straightening a small piece of wire is to put it between two steel blocks and roll them together over the wire.

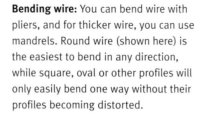

TRY IT

227 MAKE HAMMER COVERS

To keep your hammers in top condition, make protective covers for them using heavy fabric or leather. These keep them from knocking into other steel tools and will also protect them from damp.

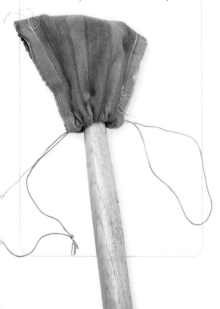

229 Making twisted wire

It is surprisingly easy to create twists in wire. It can then be used to make borders, bangles or rings, depending on the thickness of wire that you use.

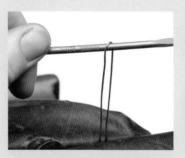

1 Take a long piece of round wire. Silver, copper or gold are best for this technique – it doesn't work as well with brass, unless it has been annealed first. Bend the piece of wire in half and put the two ends securely into a bench vice. Always overestimate the amount of wire you will need. Put a straight metal rod into the loop at the top of the wire.

2 Pull the wire upwards and begin to turn the rod around, in the same direction. The pieces of wire will begin to twist together. Keep turning until you are happy with the tightness of the twist. Take the wire out of the vice and trim the ends.

230 Making and using a bending jig

A bending jig is easy to make and can be used to create a range of jewellery pieces, all with a common theme. It will enable you to make identical earrings and other matching units with little difficulty. This jig is made of perforated steel sheets bolted together so that the holes in the sheets align. The pins are steel pop rivets. However, a piece of steel mesh fastened to a piece of drilled plywood and hard round nails will do equally well.

1 Take two sheets of 10 x 7-cm (4 x 2¾-in) perforated steel and round off the corners of both with a hand file and emery cloth. Use an electric drill with a 3-mm (⅛-in) drill bit to drill a hole in each corner.

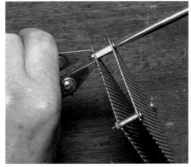

2 Assemble the two halves using four 25 x 3-mm (1 x ⅛-in) bolts with 20 nuts. Several nuts can be used to create the space between the two sheets of steel. The spacers used here are the metal inserts from electrical junction boxes.

3 Hold the jig securely in a vice. Use 3-mm (⅛-in) steel pop rivets (you may need up to 50) to mark out shapes on the jig according to your design.

4 An alternative method of making a bending jig is to drill the holes in a solid steel plate. The plate shown here is 6mm (¼in) thick. Drilling the holes is time-consuming, but you can mark them out by using a piece of perforated steel as a template and taping it to the steel plate before you start drilling.

TRY IT

231 RUBBINGS

Making a rubbing of the jig will let you work out jewellery designs on paper. Place the jig under a sheet of paper and rub over it with the side of a pencil or crayon.

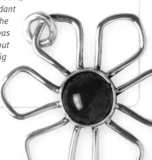

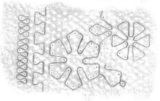

Sketch (above) and pendant (right): the design was figured out using a jig rubbing.

232 Save money – cut your own discs

Though you can buy ready-made discs in silver, copper and brass, it is an expensive option. A great alternative is to cut discs out using a disc cutter. This is a steel tool that has cut-out circles of different diameters. It can be difficult to make perfect circles by sawing, so this is an effective alternative.

1 Place your metal into the right-sized slot, in the middle of the block. Put the corresponding size of disc cutter in the hole and hit the top of the cutter very hard with a heavy steel hammer.

2 The force of the cutter through the hole will shear out the disk. This is most successful with thinner gauges of metal.

233 Dapping disks

A dapping block is a cube, made of either brass or steel, that has domes of different diameters indented on each face. The corresponding dapping punches may be made of steel or wood and have rounded ends. Use the two together to turn a metal disc into a dome.

1 Place your disc in an indentation on the dapping block of a similar diameter. Place the dapping punch that corresponds to the shape of the dome on top of the disc and, with a mallet, hammer down hard on the end of the dapping punch.

2 The punch will force the disc into the indentation to produce a dome.

234 Forging basics

Forging involves shaping metal, usually using steel hammers. As metal is hit with a steel hammer, it gets compressed and distorted. To help shape it in a controlled way, you can use formers, which are steel or wooden shapes that have the contour of the shape that you want to create in the metal. Forging can be as simple as hammering a round piece of wire with a flat-ended hammer to become the end of a head pin, or the technique may be scaled up to form an earring or bangle (see page 98).

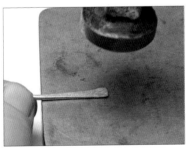

1 Place the metal to be forged on a steel block. Using a flat-ended steel hammer, strike your piece so that you begin splaying out the end of the metal, compressing it.

2 Continue to forge until you have created the look and shape that you want.

235 Making a forged open bangle

In this simple but effective bangle design, the use of forging transforms the square rod at one end of the bangle into a round rod at the other.

1 Start with a shorter piece of square rod than you need, since it gets stretched out by forging (a bangle circumference is approximately 20cm/8in). Anneal the rod, pickle and dry it. Put the rod on a steel block and use a round-ended steel hammer to hit the rod on its edges, halfway along the length. Turn it as you hammer, so that the rod is resting on its square edge, and do the same to all the other edges.

2 Remember to anneal the piece regularly. You will notice that the rod will grow in length as it is compressed into a different shape. Keep hammering until there is a gradual transformation from the square into the tapered round rod.

3 Once you are pleased with the profile of the rod, anneal it again and bend it around a bangle mandrel using a mallet. Slightly overlap the two ends and adjust the diameter of the bangle to fit.

236 Fold-forming

Fold-forming is a fairly new technique invented by Charles Lewton-Brain that produces lightweight, three-dimensional, sculptural forms. It is great for making organic shapes to be used in jewellery designs. The simplest fold to learn is the T-fold; once you have mastered this, you can progress to more complicated forms.

1 Anneal a rectangle of 0.4-mm (28-gauge) sheet metal, then bend it in half. Put the two folded ends into the bench vice, leaving the top slightly exposed. You can put leather in the vice to protect your metal. Using a mallet, tap down on the metal to flatten it. You can then start forging on top of it, using a raising hammer. You may need to anneal again if you are doing a lot of hammering.

2 Take the piece out of the vice and open out the metal. Put it on a steel block and tap the T-shape down with a mallet.

3 You can forge the edges of the metal using a raising hammer, which creates a rippled edge to the metal.

Creating a multi-fold piece

237

This technique is experimental, so it can be hard to plan and repeat exactly. It will require some practice to create satisfying and useful shapes, but in time you will be able to produce some amazing organic forms.

1 Fold a piece of thin annealed metal in half and hammer it flat with a mallet. Put the piece of metal into a bench vice, with the folded side in the jaws. Pry open the pieces of metal and flatten them using a mallet.

2 Take the piece of metal out of the vice and fold the pieces that are at right angles down farther.

3 Fully flatten the folded pieces on a steel block using a mallet.

4 Repeat steps 1, 2 and 3 twice more. This will create more and more folds within the metal.

5 Put the metal on its side on the steel block and, using a raising hammer, hammer along the folded edge; this will make the edge spread out as it is hit. Anneal the piece occasionally, to keep the metal from becoming brittle.

6 Finally, when you are pleased with the curve that the hammering has created, open the piece up. You may need to use a thin metal object to slide into the folds to help you open them up. You will have created a curved, sculptural, organic form.

Fold-formed pendant
This pendant uses folded silver. You could also create earrings and bangles using the multi-fold technique.

238 Anticlastic raising

'Anticlastic' means having a curvature in two opposite directions at any given point. Anticlastic raising therefore involves shaping sheet metal into three-dimensional shapes with undulating forms, forcing the metal to go in different directions. To achieve this, you will need a specialist tool called a sinusoidal stake – a wiggly steel stake that has different curvatures to shape the metal against; you will also need a nylon hammer, which won't mark the metal. The hammer forces the metal into the indentations on the stake into directions that you want. The metal doesn't naturally want to go in two directions, so it has to be forced into the curves by stretching it with the compression of the hammer's action. The tools used are simple; it is your technique and skill that make the metal move in the directions that you want.

Sinusoidal stake
This piece of equipment is used for shaping metal into concave forms.

239 Making an anticlastic bangle

Make a sheet metal bangle of your chosen width, using metal no thicker than 0.8mm (20 gauge). The bangle can be straight-sided or made with curved edges to it.

1 Clamp the sinusoidal stake firmly into a bench vice, horizontally. Begin shaping the bangle with a round-ended mallet.

2 Slip the bangle over the stake so that it is sitting on the largest curve. Holding it in the middle of the curve, use the nylon hammer and hit it in the centre to start to push the centre of the bangle inwards. Repeat this action all the way around the bangle or where you want it to curve inwards.

240 Improvising with dapping punches

This method allows you to make an anticlastic curve without using a sinusoidal stake. First you need to make the two rings. Make the first ring in 0.8-mm (20-gauge) sheet metal, about 10mm (³⁄₈in) wide – or, use a ready-made plain ring band. Make a wire ring out of 1-mm (18-gauge) round wire that will easily slide over the sheet metal ring, then polish both rings (see pages 106–108).

1 Put a large dapping punch, about 2.5cm (1in) in diameter, into a bench vice facing upwards. Now place the sheet metal ring on top of it and slip over the wire ring.

2 Place the second dapping punch on top of the ring and tap down on it with a mallet. This will force the punches down into the ring, splaying out the edges and trapping the wire ring on the ring band. The wire ring should be able to spin freely, but not come off the ring.

3 Anneal and pickle the bangle and continue onto a smaller-sized curve. If you want to make the inward curve more extreme, keep going until you achieve the effect you are looking for.

3 There are different variations you can make on this ring design. You could use a plain or textured ring band – the texturing would need to be done before you make it into a ring – or you could put designs on the wire ring.

BEGINNERS START HERE!
241 Casting basics

Casting is the technique of pouring molten metal into a mould, which creates a three-dimensional form. Traditionally, metal casting was done by the 'lost wax' process. You first create an object in wax by carving or turning it on a lathe, to create your design. You can buy wax for carving from specialist suppliers, and it comes in different hardnesses. It also comes in various shapes such as blocks, ring blanks or in sheet form, and what you choose will depend on what you are planning to make.

To carve wax, you will need some steel carving tools. Also useful are wax saw blades and a wax heat pen, to help cut and mould the wax. Carving wax models is a skilled technique and will take a bit of practice. If you cut a piece of wax off by mistake, it can be rejoined using heat.

Once you have carved the wax model, you need a mould for the metal to be poured into. Moulds can be made from different materials, including casting sand and investment plaster. In a home workshop, casting sand is the most suitable; it is a type of mouldable sand that molten metal can be poured directly into.

Pewter casting is a good introduction to casting and is achievable in a small workshop with basic tools. Pewter has a low melting temperature and is relatively affordable. It also polishes up well to give a finish similar to silver. Pewter can't be silver soldered, but pewter solder is available from specialist suppliers. You will have to think about incorporating fittings, either by riveting or by embedding them in the molten metal.

242 OUTSOURCE YOUR CASTING

FIX IT

If you want a piece cast in gold, silver or bronze, remember that these metals will need to be heated to a very high temperature to melt them. If you don't have a torch that reaches such a high temperature, you can send your wax or metal model to a specialist casting company. They will make a mould, create the sprue (where the metal gets poured in and the air escapes from the mould) and cast the piece in the metal of your choice. Once they have made your mould, you can order as many pieces as you want and in whatever metal you want. This may be worth doing if you want to repeat a design element or are intending to make a lot of the same pieces. When you get the piece back from the casting company there will be little stumps left on it; these are the remainders of the sprues and will need to be sawn off, filed and sanded.

Casting stages
From top to bottom: a plastic prototype used to create a mould, the silver casting created from that mould and a finished use of the casting on a pendant.

243 Pewter ammonite pendant

This project includes making a one-part mould to make a flat-backed object. It is possible to make a two-part mould in a similar way, which is completely three-dimensional. You don't have to use an ammonite – many other small objects would work.

Pewter castings
Pewter casting and the ammonite they were made from (top), showing the accuracy of the reproduction.

HEALTH AND SAFETY

Be very aware that molten metal can burn you badly. The best place to melt metal is on a metal draining board in the kitchen, because you are next to water and the surface of the draining board isn't flammable. Make sure there is nothing flammable close by, particularly curtains. Wear sensible shoes and protect your hands with gardening or leather gloves, but make sure you can still handle things easily.

1 Tightly pack Delft casting sand into a cookie cutter, hammer it down with a mallet and scrape the sand level with the top of the cutter.

2 Dig out a small indentation for the ammonite to go into and push it into the sand, level with the surface of the cutter or as deep as you want your pendant to be. Then remove it carefully, so as not to disturb the sand too much, and gently remove any excess sand from the mould.

3 Place the pewter casting bar in the crucible and put this on top of the heat-proof block. Light your torch and start heating the pewter. It will start to melt very quickly.

4 Once it is fully molten, very carefully pour it into the mould, making sure you don't overfill it, otherwise you will have to remove the excess pewter. Leave it for a minute to let it solidify.

5 Remove the pewter with tweezers and quench it in water, then dry it and drill a hole (see page 103) near the top to put a jump ring through. Remove any sharp edges with sandpaper.

6 Polish the piece with a brass brush or on a wheel (see pages 106–107), or even leave it just as it is. If you are unhappy with the result, you can re-melt the pewter and repeat the process.

Drilling

Drilling can be used to make a hole to thread wire through to hang a pendant or to put a saw blade through for piercing out; it can also be used in a decorative way, to create a pattern. The keys to good drilling are accurate measurement and consideration of what the hole you are drilling is actually for.

Decorative drilling
This antique Norwegian brooch features drilled holes as decoration.

244 Drilling a hole

Think about the diameter of the hole you want – this will influence the size of drill bit you choose. If it's for linking pieces of metal together with a jump ring, make sure that the hole is a little bigger than the diameter of wire you are going to pass through it, so that the pieces of metal have plenty of room to move.

1 Measure accurately where you are going to make the hole. Make sure that it is not too close to the edge of the metal, but also not too far in – especially if the hole is for a jump ring to go through. Use a punch and a mallet to tap a light indentation into the metal; this is to locate the drill bit. The type of drill bit will depend on the type of drill you are using (see page 104 for details on which drill is best for your purposes).

2 Clamp the piece of metal down or hold it in a ring clamp. It is best not to hold the metal with just your hands, because it may spin and cut you. Attach the drill bit you have selected and hold the drill in an upright position at 90 degrees to the metal, located in the indentation you made on the metal. You will need to apply slight downward pressure – but not too hard, otherwise you may break the bit. If the drill bit is sharp, it should go through the metal quickly.

BE SAFE

Always wear goggles when drilling metal.

245 WHAT IF THE HOLES ARE TOO SMALL?

FIX IT

If you've drilled a hole that's too small, you can enlarge it using a round needle file. Put the file into the hole as far as it will go and then rotate it, so that it reams the hole out to a larger size.

TRY IT

246 MAKE BITS AND BURRS LAST LONGER

To make your drill bits and burrs last, you can buy custom products to lubricate them and keep them sharper for longer. You can also use wax for a similar effect.

247 Know your bit size

It is useful to have a large selection of different-sized drill bits, because you never know in advance what you will need. The problem is that the sizes are no longer written on the shaft of the bit, so once you have taken them out of their packaging it can be difficult to see the difference between drill bits. Either mark the size yourself on each drill bit, or keep different sizes in separate boxes. You can also buy magnetic holders for drill bits, which can be a useful way of keeping the different sizes of bit separate.

248 Getting the best out of each type of drill

These are the most popular drills available. Your selection will depend on what you plan to use it for, it could be just for drilling holes or perhaps to set stone. Whatever your needs, there will be one to suit your budget.

Bow drill

A bow drill is a very traditional tool and it can be very effective if used properly.

How to use: Screw the drill bit into the collet, hold the drill at 90 degrees to the metal, then twist the shaft of the drill while holding the handle. This will twist the cord around the top of the shaft. Hold the handle on either side and gently push down. When the handle reaches the bottom and the cord unwinds, it will make the handle rise up again. This should be a continuous action: it works on a similar principle to a spinning top – momentum keeps it going.

Archimedes drill

This is a very simple, ancient mechanism for drilling holes.

How to use: Screw the drill bit into the collet and hold it at 90 degrees to the metal. Push down on the top, which will start the drill bit spinning around. Keep pushing it up and down until it slowly drills through the metal.

Hobby drill

This drill is useful if you want to do more than just drill holes, but also want to use burrs and polishing attachments. Some of these types of drills come with different-sized collets, which you have to change for use with different-diameter drill bits or burrs. The best kind to choose is a drill with an adjustable collet, which means you don't have to keep changing the collet for different attachments.

How to use: Fit your drill bit into the collet and hold it at 90 degrees to the metal. The drill may have an adjustable speed control; if it does, select a fairly slow speed for drilling and apply a little pressure.

Pendant drill

These drills are relatively expensive, but are designed especially for jewellers; their big advantages are the foot pedal control and the slim hand piece. It is best to buy one with an adjustable collet. The foot pedal keeps your hands free when the drill starts up.

How to use: Set the drill up next to your workbench, either with the motor hanging on a hook or on a clamped-on stand on the workbench. Screw the drill bit into the collet. Make sure you have tightened the collet properly and – very important – have removed the key before you start the drill, otherwise it will jam the motor. Put the drill bit at 90 degrees to the metal, then press down lightly on the foot pedal of the drill to start drilling.

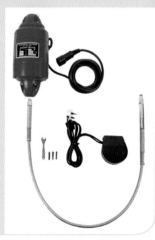

Finishing and polishing

Polishing, particularly on silver, can completely transform a piece of jewellery. However, to create a high mirror shine takes a lot of time; the best way to minimize the work is to avoid scratching pieces during the making process. Jewellery doesn't have to be shiny, though. There are many other possible surface finishes and decorative effects that you can use to vary the look and feel of a piece of jewellery.

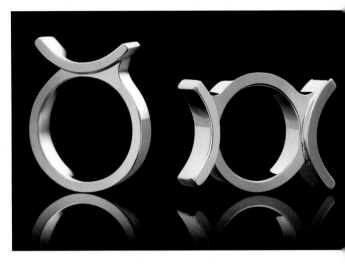

High-shine finishing
These silver rings have a wonderful mirror-shine finish.

Once you have finished soldering a piece, it can often look less than perfect; it may seem impossible that it will ever look like a proper piece of jewellery. Finishing is a part of the process that is often overlooked: to get a professional finish takes time. How a piece is constructed will govern when you need to sand and polish it. For example, you may need to

polish the piece completely before you assemble it, which would be the case with hinged, stone-set and riveted items. Begin with sanding – to get a good finish, you have to create scratches in order to remove deeper ones. A good way of telling where you need to sand is to feel the piece of jewellery for any rough or sharp edges that need to be removed.

Sanding basics

249

Sandpapers are graded by their coarseness; generally, the higher the number written on the back, the finer the sandpaper.

- Use fine sandpaper (try 240-grit) to start to remove the deeper scratches; it makes it easier to hold the sandpaper if you wrap it around a small block of wood or a needle file of the right profile.This helps to preserve the profile of the metal and avoids rounding off any of the edges.
- Try not to sand over areas that you have textured either with hammers or a rolling mill, otherwise you may remove the texture.

- Once you have removed deep scratches and any firestain from the piece, you can move to a finer grade and then continue down the grades, removing the scratches that were made on the last pass, until the piece is ready to polish on a wheel.
- There are specialist finishing materials to help you 'sand' in difficult places, such as abrasive strings and tapes that can get into awkward areas that sandpaper can't reach. These also come in different grades. Abrasive sponge pads are great for sanding contours.

250 Polishing by hand

Polishing by hand is a way of achieving a high polish. It is sometimes more suitable and invariably safer than machine polishing.

For delicate items, such as the scroll shown here, you can sprinkle jeweller's rouge onto a felt pad and rub it over the piece. A scrap of carpet will serve the purpose if felt is not available.

You can also use powdered rouge with the suede side of a piece of scrap leather, a polishing cloth or a soft cloth.

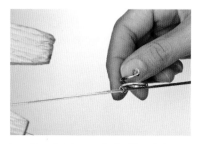

Lengths of string coated with polish are also useful. Secure one end to the bench, then thread awkward items onto one or more strands and rub them back and forth along the tightly held string.

251 Picking a mop and polish for your wheel

If you would rather not polish by hand, you can use a polishing wheel. The polishing motor turns spindles that the polishing mops are attached to. It is easy to change the mop and there are lots of different types and shapes available. Here is a list of some different types of mop available and what you might use them for.

FUNCTION OR FINISH	MOP	POLISH
Basic	Calico mops: stitched (harder) or unstitched (softer)	Tripoli polish
Final	Swansdown, reflex, wool or felt mops	Rouge polish
Matte, scratched finish	Scotch-Brite wheel	No polish
Satin or matte finish	Frosting wheels	No polish
Polishing inside rings	Finger felts	Tripoli polish

Polishing mops
Clockwise from left: calico, reflex and Scotch-Brite mops.

252 REMOVING SCRATCHES

Remove scratches on the surface of metal with a scraper made from an old file or hacksaw blade (below left) – a penknife blade can be used as a scraper. Always scrape along the scratch, not across it.

You can also use a burnisher (below right) to remove scratches in much the same way as the scraper. A burnisher works in a similar way to a planishing hammer, imparting a polish by rubbing the hard, polished metal over the surface of the softer metal. Burnishing is often the only means of hardening work after soldering.

FIX IT

BEGINNERS START HERE!

253 How to polish on a wheel

Using a polishing wheel will help you to achieve a high-shine finish. However, if you're not happy with the result, you can repeat any of the processes again, right back to the beginning with sandpaper, if you can still see scratches on the metal. If the piece you are polishing is pulled out of your hands while polishing, make sure you turn off the motor and let the wheel stop before you retrieve it from under the bench.

HEALTH AND SAFETY

Always wear goggles and tie up your hair when polishing on a wheel. Don't wear a scarf or have anything dangling near the wheel. Don't try to polish tiny items or chains on a wheel.

1 Attach a stitched calico mop to the polishing motor's spindle and a felt mop (or similar) to the other spindle. Turn on the motor, apply Tripoli to the calico mop, and hold it against the wheel for about two seconds, following the movement of the wheel. This should be enough polish to start with – it is better to add little and often.

2 Hold the piece firmly in both hands and place it against the bottom half of the wheel – never on the top half, because the piece will be pulled out of your hands. This will start to polish the piece. Move it around a little and use the edge of the wheel to polish into corners. Once the piece is polished all over, turn off the motor.

3 Wash the piece with soapy water to remove excess polish and dry it. Put some rouge onto the final polishing mop and repeat polishing on this side; the final polish should bring the piece up to a high shine. Wash again to remove excess polish.

254 Refining using burrs

Different types of burrs are available for use in pendant and hobby drills. These are really useful for removing blobs of excess solder or a blemish in just one spot, because you can target small areas rather than sanding across the whole item. They come in different shapes and grades, so do make sure you buy ones that are meant for jewellery; other burrs available will be too harsh. You need to be careful when using burrs not to linger in one spot on the metal, since they can create indentations if left there too long. Once you have removed the blemish, you can resume using sandpaper to remove the marks created by the burr.

TRY IT

255 POLISHING ATTACHMENTS FOR DRILLS

You can get small versions of polishing mops and burrs for sanding, to use as attachments in drills, and these will give a similar effect to the polishing wheel (use the same kinds of polish). You can clamp your drill sideways into a vice so that both your hands are free to polish the piece.

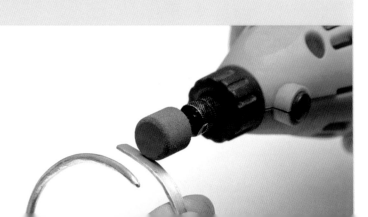

256 Barrel polishing

If you don't have a proper workshop set-up and space is limited, or you are going to make a lot of chains, a barrel polisher is a good solution. It is cleaner than using a polishing wheel and does save time, although the finish is not as good.

Put stainless-steel shot inside the barrel and cover it with water, then add a pinch of cleaning compound, which comes as a powder. Don't use too much, because it can make an enormous amount of foam. Put your pieces of jewellery into the barrel. Don't overload it – ten pendants is a rough guide, but this will depend on the capacity of your barrel polisher.

If you are polishing hollow items, it's worth plugging holes in the pieces with cork or another similar material, otherwise they may be filled with steel shot.

1 Fasten the lid on the barrel and put it onto the rollers. Turn it on. It then rotates, making the stainless-steel shot rub against the jewellery; this action is what burnishes and polishes the metal.

2 Leave it rotating for about one hour, then check on the pieces and see how shiny they are. Continue for longer if necessary.

TRY IT

258 CREATING A SATIN FINISH

Some pieces of jewellery, especially textured pieces, don't suit having a very shiny surface. You can use a brass wire bristle brush to apply a satin finish (keep it moving in the same direction for a more even finish). You can also buy a brass brush as an attachment for a drill; if you use one of these, make sure you wear protective goggles. If you would like a more matte look, you can make circular motions with a metal pan scourer for an interesting scratched finish. Scotch-Brite mops used on a polishing wheel will give a similar effect.

257 Patination and oxidation

Patinating and oxidizing are interesting finishes that you can give your jewellery. They are achieved using different chemicals, depending on which finish you want. Either can add a different dimension to a piece of jewellery. Antiquing (right) is popular for silver, while verdigris (opposite) can transform copper or bronze.

Antiqued pendant
The liver of sulfur has successfully antiqued the lettering, making it really stand out.

259 Antiquing with liver of sulphur

Liver of sulphur is a chemical you can use to antique silver by making it turn black, which looks especially striking on textured pieces. You can also achieve a range of colours, including blues and greens.

Mix up the liver of sulphur – it can come as crystals, a gel or powder and is usually made into a solution with warm water. Read the manufacturer's instructions carefully. Wear rubber gloves, since it can stain your hands. Dip your piece of silver into the solution using plastic tweezers. Once you achieve the colours you want, remove the piece from the solution and dip it into neutralizing solution (water and a tablespoon of baking soda) for one minute to stop

TRY IT

260 USING PLATINOL

You can get similar effects to using liver of sulphur by using Platinol. The main difference is that Platinol comes ready mixed as a liquid, which can be used cold. It only turns silver black and does not produce the variety of colours that you can get with liver of sulphur. The other difference is that it is painted on with a brush, which instantly turns the silver black. This also means that you can be selective in where you want to use it, because it doesn't have to be dipped. Paint it on the area you want to make black, leave it to dry, then use a silver cloth or light sandpaper to polish off the raised areas if desired.

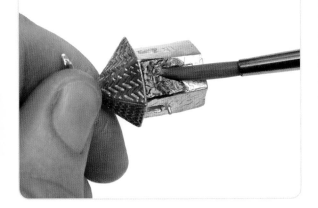

261 Heat treating copper and bronze

You can give copper and bronze interesting surface finishes by lightly heating them. This oxidizes the surface, and you can create an amazing array of colours such as reds and purples this way. Place your piece of copper on a soldering block, then light the torch and heat the surface of the metal. You will see the metal changing colour. When you notice the colour change, turn off the torch, pick up the metal with tweezers and quench it in cold water. Don't pickle the piece, because you will lose all the colours. To seal the colours you can either wax the piece or use matte car spray varnish on it.

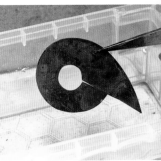

the action of the chemicals. Now dry the piece.

Use a silver cloth or polishing pads to rub over the piece of jewellery. This will take off the patina on the raised areas and leave it in the indentations. This gives a three-dimensional look and highlights the textures of the piece.

Colour range
You can achieve yellows, greens and blues on a silver surface using liver of sulphur.

Colouring the silver
Make sure you use plastic tweezers when dipping the silver in the liver of sulphur solution.

TRY IT

262 TURNING COPPER GREEN

The green on copper is known as verdigris. You can buy proprietary chemicals to paint on with a brush or you can simply use vinegar and salt. A way to get a more even green colour is to put sawdust soaked in the proprietary chemical in a plastic bag and leave the piece in it for a few days. You can use this method for bronze as well. Always wear protective gloves.

TRY IT

263 PRINTING ALUMINIUM

This is a simple technique, using a rubber stamp, for finishing aluminium by colouring it. Once you have mastered it, you could move onto more adventurous printing techniques, such as linocutting or screen printing.

1 Take the sheet of uncoloured, anodized aluminium 1.8mm (14 gauge) and remove the paper it's wrapped in, being careful not to touch the surface, since the oil from your fingers will resist any dye. Use a permanent pen to colour in the pattern on the rubber stamp.

2 Quickly print the rubber stamp onto the surface of the metal before it dries out. (It's worth practising this beforehand, on a piece of paper.)

Printed and dyed kilt pin
After printing and dying, the aluminium was sawn into shape, pierced and attached to a kilt pin.

3 Put on some rubber gloves. Fill a plastic container with your chosen colour of dye, then take the piece of aluminium (use tweezers to avoid touching the surface) and dip it into the dye. The longer it's submerged in the dye, the deeper the colour you will achieve.

4 Once you're happy with the colour, remove the metal with the tweezers and wash it under the tap, then let it dry. Put a pan of water on to boil, with a colander inside just above the level of the water. Place the aluminium in the colander.

Note Anodized aluminium is very resilient and so doesn't lend itself well to too much bending.

5 Put the lid of the pan on and allow it to steam for 30–40 minutes. Don't let it boil dry. This will seal the surface of the aluminium and make the dye permanent. Leave to cool.

6 Take the cooled aluminum out of the pan. You can touch the surface now, because it is sealed. Cut out the design and shape and finish the aluminium.

264 Keum boo

Keum boo is an ancient Korean metalworking technique that fuses pure gold leaf to pure silver; it's a stronger bond than just plating and it won't wear off. It's very striking and uses a tiny amount of gold to good effect.

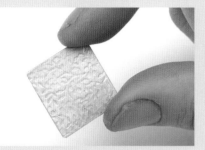

1 It's easier to fuse the gold leaf to the fine silver if the design is fairly flat and the metal not too thick. Prepare your piece of fine silver by soldering any design or fittings you want onto it. You could add a light texture to the surface with the rolling mill, since keum boo gold leaf takes on any contours on the surface of the silver. Make sure your piece of silver is very clean before you start.

2 The gold leaf comes inside pieces of paper. It's best left inside these when you are cutting out the shape you want. Use scissors or a craft knife to cut out the shape from the keum boo gold leaf, then carefully remove the gold leaf from the paper and place it where you want it fused on the silver.

3 Place the piece on a hotplate and turn it on to full power. Wait for the hot plate to reach 260°C–370°C (500°F–700°F). Be careful not to blow the gold off the silver, and wear heat-protective gloves while you work. Hold the silver still with a pair of tweezers and in your other hand use a burnisher to rub over the gold leaf, concentrating on the edges. Apply fairly heavy pressure all over, trying not to tear the foil or get air bubbles under it, until it starts to stick to the surface of the silver. If you do tear the gold, you can patch over the top with another piece. When the gold looks as if it is at the same level as the silver, this usually means that it has fused. Take it off the hotplate with tweezers and let it cool. You can then check how well the gold leaf has adhered; if it is still loose, repeat the process.

4 A satin finish works well on keum boo, because it shows off the contrast of the gold and silver better than a high shine. You can achieve this by using a brass brush (see page 108). The brass brush will also help you see if the gold has adhered properly.

Keum boo works because gold and silver have similar structures, so will exchange molecules at a temperature below their usual soldering temperature to produce a permanent bond.

Keum boo rings
These 'Landscape rings' by Felicity Peters make use of keum boo to great effect.

All about stones

Stones are great for adding colour and sparkle to your jewellery designs. The information and guidance in this section will help you decide which stones and settings are right for your piece. Stones can be used as the centrepiece of a design or as an accent.

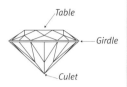

Faceted stone from above

Faceted stone side view

Cabochon side view

265 Stones to start with

When you begin setting stones it's best to start with round ones, because the settings are easier to make, then move on to ovals. Any stone settings that have corners are harder to make.

267 Cabochon and faceted cuts

There are essentially two types of cut: cabochon is flat-bottomed with a rounded top, while faceted stones have facets cut into the faces and a pointed bottom. A faceted cut is usually chosen for transparent stones in order to accentuate their sparkle. There are many variations within these two main cut types.

266 Selecting your stone: shape

Here are the most common stone shapes available. They are not all available for all stones and they generally come in standard sizes. You may buy a stone and decide to make your jewellery design around it; its shape, size, cut and depth will affect what you can make it into and what type of setting you can use for it.

TRILLION

PEAR

ROUND

OVAL

CUSHION

BAGUETTE

MARQUISE

EMERALD CUT

HEART

TRIANGULAR

The chart below will help you choose which stones to use, based on colour. It also gives you an indication of how expensive they are.

White/clear	Pearl ** C
	Rock crystal * C and F
	Opal *** C
	Diamond *** F
	Quartz * F
	Moonstone * C
Yellow	Lemon quartz * C and F
	Citrine * C and F
	Amber * C
	Yellow sapphire *** C and F
Orange	Amber * C
	Sunstone ** C and F
	Mandarin citrine ** C and F
Red	Garnet * C and F
	Carnelian * C
	Red spinel *** C and F
	Ruby *** C and F
Pink	Rose quartz * C
	Pink tourmaline *** C and F
	Rhodolite * C and F
	Pink sapphire *** C and F
Purple	Amethyst ** C and F
	Iolite ** C and F
	Fluorite * C
	Sugulite ** C
	Tanzanite *** F
	Purple sapphire *** F

Blue	Blue topaz ** C and F
	Lapis lazuli ** C
	Sapphire *** C and F
	Blue moonstone ** C
	Aquamarine *** C and F
	Blue tourmaline *** C and F
	Turquoise * C
	Opal *** C
Green	Malachite * C
	Jade ** C
	Green tourmaline ** C and F
	Emerald *** C and F
	Peridot ** C and F
	Tsavorite ** C and F
Brown	Smoky quartz * C and F
	Tiger's eye * C
	Agate * C
Black	Black onyx * C
	Hematite * C
	Jet ** C

KEY

* to *** = *least to most expensive*

F = *faceted*

C = *cabochon*

Aquamarine ring
This emerald-cut stone has been set in white gold by Baxter Moerman Jewellery.

269 Selecting your stone: hardness

The Mohs Scale is designed to show the hardness of stones, with 1 being the softest up to 10, the hardest – diamond. Particularly for ring designs, it helps to choose a harder stone that is less likely to chip with heavy wear.

The Mohs Scale

1 Talc
2 Gypsum – amber
3 Calcite – pearl
4 Fluorite – malachite
5 Apatite – turquoise, lapis lazuli
6 Feldspar – opal, hematite, moonstone, sunstone, sugulite
7 Quartz – tourmaline, iolite, amethyst, citrine, garnet, peridot, tiger's eye, black onyx, tanzanite
8 Topaz – spinel, emerald, aquamarine
9 Corundum – sapphire, ruby
10 Diamond

270 Setting types

A stone setting is a way of keeping a stone in place on a piece of jewellery. This can be achieved in many different ways, with a traditional or a non-traditional setting. Some traditional stone settings are only suitable for certain shapes or cuts of stones, but you can also devise more unorthodox ways of setting a stone. The most important features of any stone setting are that it keeps the stone securely in place and that it is suitable for the cut and stone type.

Here is a list of traditional stone settings and their level of difficulty. Cabochon stones are generally easier to set than faceted ones, so are good to start off with.

Setting Name		Setting description
Bezel		Most commonly used for cabochon stones, but can also be for faceted; can be straight-sided or tapered. *
Flush		For small, usually round, faceted stones set into the metal to be level with the surface, so they seem to be invisibly set. ***
Claw		Usually used for faceted stones; either four or six claws hold the stone in place. **
Tension		For faceted stones that are high on the Mohs Scale, stones are set into concealed notches and are held in place by the tension of the metal. ***
Pavé		Faceted stones are put into countersunk holes and held in place with small grains of metal. ***
Channel or bar		Baguette-cut, round or square faceted stones are set into a channel of metal; often used on rings to create a line of stones. ***

KEY   *= Easy   **= Moderate   ***= Difficult

271 Specialist stone-setting tools

To start using stones in your jewellery designs, there are some special tools that you will need for the job. They are often not expensive and you can build your collection as you expand your range of techniques. To begin with, a bezel pusher and burnisher are the main tools you'll require.

- **Bezel pusher** A bulbous-ended steel tool used for pushing the bezel over onto a stone.
- **Burnisher** A pointed, smooth, steel tool used for burnishing the metal onto the stone.
- **Collet block** A heavy steel block with tapered indentations, with a corresponding shaped punch, used to shape settings into a tapered collet instead of a straight-sided bezel. These come in different shapes, such as round, oval and pear-shaped.

- **Stone-setting burrs** Steel attachments for drills, used to burr out metal to make a stone fit into a setting.
- **Stone-setting mandrels** These are miniature versions of a ring mandrel; they come in a variety of shapes and are used to shape the bezel.
- **Magnifying headband** A magnifying device worn on the head that is very useful when you are setting a stone.
- **Jeweller's loupe** A magnifying hand-held device used to see whether the stone is set successfully.
- **Digital micrometer** A very useful tool if you are going to do a lot of stone setting, it gives a digital display of the exact measurement of a stone or setting.

272 Making a bezel setting

This method shows you how to make a simple setting for a cabochon stone, using a fine silver bezel strip. It is made from fine silver and not sterling silver, which means that it is very soft and bendy. You can buy it in strips either 3mm (⅛in) or 5mm (³⁄₁₆in) wide, and it is usually used for fairly small cabochon stones. Because the strip is soft, this helps to make it easier to push over the stone to set it. You can also use strips of sterling silver sheet, though this is more difficult to bend over the stone because it is harder metal.

You can buy bearer wire to help you set cabochon stones. This is a strip of silver with a built-in ledge on it, which is what the stone rests on; it also gives you an open back to the setting, which lets the light through the stone, amplifying its sparkle.

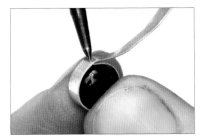

1 Use a needle file to create a right angle at the end of a 3mm x 10cm (⅛in x 4in) silver bezel strip. Place a round cabochon stone on a flat surface and wrap the bezel strip around the bottom edge of the stone. If it is a good fit, you should be able to pick up the stone using the bezel strip; it is important that it fits tightly around the bottom.

2 Where the bezel strip overlaps, make an accurate mark with a scriber.

3 Cut the strip larger than you need using side cutters. File the ends of the strip at a right angle, up to the scribed line. Check that the bezel fits around the bottom of the stone. Get the two ends of the strip to fit closely together. Flux the seam and place a fluxed piece of solder at the bottom of the seam, making sure that it touches both sides of the seam. Think about what the bezel is going to be soldered onto and how many times you will be soldering. If you are only soldering a couple of times, use medium solder.

4 Use a very small flame, because it is very easy to overheat the bezel and melt it. Heat it evenly until the solder has run and joined it together. Put the bezel into the pickle to clean it.

5 Take the bezel out of the pickle, dry it and place it on a small round mandrel. Tap it gently with a mallet to make it round. Check that the bezel still fits the stone. Use a flat needle file to file the seam; also sand it so that the seam completely disappears.

6 You can now solder it onto your piece of jewellery or solder it onto a piece of silver to make a backing for the stone, then saw around the edge of the setting and file the edges, so that the seam disappears.

FIX IT

273 BEZEL TOO SMALL?

If your bezel is a little too small for your stone, you can try stretching it slightly on a mandrel, using a mallet. If it is too big, you will have to cut a sliver out and re-solder it.

274 Making the bezel the right height

When you have soldered the setting onto your design, you need to check that the height of the bezel is right for your particular stone. Every cabochon stone has a different curve on top; some are quite shallow and some are quite domed. You need to measure, with a pair of dividers, the height at which the stone starts to curve in, then make a mark with a scriber very slightly above this measurement. If the measurement is too low, the stone will not have enough metal to secure it, but if the measurement is too high the silver will crumple as you push it over.

Full height bezel setting for a high-domed stone.

Depth that the bezel must be to fit this stone.

A shallower stone will require a shallower bezel.

Perfect bezel setting. The dome of the stone sits just above the bezel.

FIX IT

275 BEZEL DISTORTION

When you have the measurement correctly marked on the side of the bezel, use a flat needle file to bring the bezel down to this line, making sure you file it level. Filing often distorts the bezel, however, so when you have got it to the right height, remove any burrs from the edge (see page 78) and straighten up the edges of the setting by going around the inside with a straight-edged tool.

276 Setting a stone into a bezel

Once you have the correct height for your bezel, you are ready to set the stone in it. Sand and polish the bezel first – the stone setting itself is almost the last process.

1 Use the end of a burnisher to slightly push out the edges of the bezel to make sure the stone can easily drop into it. A piece of adhesive putty or sticky tape is useful for moving the stone in and out of the setting; this helps you to put it in level and not jam it into the bezel at a difficult angle. Lightly push down on the stone; you should feel when it contacts the bottom of the setting.

2 Using a bezel pusher, lightly push against the bezel, which will start to bend over the curve of the stone. It is better to do lots of small movements rather than one big push, which can cause the bezel to kink. Go around the stone a few times to get the bezel to close up against the stone.

3 Use a burnisher to go around the bezel again; this burnishes the silver against the stone, giving you a neat finish. Be careful not to slip over the top of the stone and scratch it.

TRY IT

277 CLAMPING YOUR RING

You may prefer to clamp your piece of jewellery in a bench vice or ring clamp so that it can't move too much while the stone is being set. Or you can use masking tape to fix it onto the bench.

278 The advantages of ready-made settings

Making settings can be time consuming and technically difficult, so there is a wide array of different shapes and sizes of settings available to buy. These can save time, although they can also limit your design possibilities. One advantage of a ready-made setting is that you know exactly what size of stone is going to fit. You just need to solder the setting onto your jewellery design and set the stone.

Ready-made silver setting
A faceted peridot in a ready-made setting soldered onto a ring.

Bezel cup for cabochons

Bezel for faceted stone to be set from behind

Snap-tite claw settings for faceted stones

Setting for a square cabochon stone

279 Cheaper alternatives to ready-made settings

You can use ready-made tubing to make settings for stones. This is generally for round stones, although you can also buy square tubing to set square stones. Tubing works well for both cabochon and faceted stones. It is a much cheaper alternative to buying ready-made settings, but requires just a little more work and technical ability.

• **Choosing the right size tubing** You will need thick-walled tubing. You need the outside diameter of the tube to be larger than the diameter of your stone and the inside diameter to be smaller. So, for example, for setting a 5mm (³/₁₆in) round faceted stone you would use tubing with an outside diameter of 5.5mm (⁷/₃₂in) and an inside diameter of 4.2mm (⁶/₃₂in), so the thickness of the tube is 0.65mm. You will need a 5mm (³/₁₆in) stone-setting burr to create a ledge for the stone to sit on. You can

do this for both faceted and cabochon stones. If you create a ledge for a cabochon stone, it means that your setting will be higher than if it was sitting flush to the bottom of the tube.
• **Making a tube setting for a faceted stone** You need to create a shaped ledge for the stone to sit on, because of the pointed shape of the bottom of a faceted stone. You can create this using a stone-setting burr of the right size for the stone, in a drill.

Gold tube setting
A tourmaline in a gold tube setting on a reticulated disk.

Silver tube setting
Cabochon sapphire set in an open-backed silver tube with a ledge inside.

280 Making your tube setting

This is an example of a tube setting to create a pair of earrings with faceted stones.
This setting can be used in any piece of jewellery that you can solder tubing onto.

1 Saw off a piece of the tubing, longer than you need. File the ends of the tube at right angles, or shape one end depending on what it is going to be soldered onto. For example, if the tube is going to be soldered onto a ring, you need to file the bottom of the tube to match the profile of the ring.

2 Solder the tubing onto your chosen design and pickle it. File the top edge of the tubing at a right angle and to the height you want the setting. Make sure that it is higher than the depth of the stone. You may want to pierce out the back of the setting with a drill to allow light to shine through, particularly for earring designs.

3 Clamp the piece into a vice, then fit the stone-setting burr in the electric drill. If your drill has a speed control, choose a slow speed. The technique of burring out a ledge is easier to do with a pendant drill, because you have both hands free. You may find it easier to see what is happening if you wear magnifying goggles.

4 Put the stone-setting burr into the end of the tubing, hold it firmly in position and turn on the drill. Burr out the inside edge of the tube to create a ledge. The key is getting the height and level of the ledge correct, so that the girdle (widest part) of the stone fits inside the tube, just below the level of the top of the tubing, leaving just enough metal to push over the stone.

5 If you burr too deep and the table (top) of the stone is lower than the top of the tube, you can file the top of the tubing off, as long as the culet (bottom point) of the stone will still fit in the setting. Use a piece of adhesive putty to pick up the stone and place it in the setting. If the shelf is uneven, it will make the stone tip in one direction.

6 Once you are happy that the stone is sitting correctly, use either a bezel pusher or a burnisher to trap the stone in position by pushing onto the metal. Push first at north, then south, east then west. Be careful not to push the stone out of the setting with the first push. Once it is trapped you can carry on with a burnisher, pushing the metal down all around the circumference of the setting so that it is tight up to the stone.

Studs with tube-set stones
These peridots have been set in silver tubes and soldered onto a textured silver backing.

281 USING A COLLET BLOCK TO MAKE A TAPERED SETTING

If you use tubing to make a stone setting, it is straight sided. However, it can be nice to taper the setting, which can make it more elegant. A simple way of achieving this is using a collet block and punch, with tubing. Make sure that the tubing that you use is unsoldered and without seams.

1 Cut a length of tube for your setting; its outside diameter needs to be the same size as the stone you want to set. Put the piece of tube into one of the indents in the collet block, so that the top of the tube is smaller than the diameter of the collet indent.

2 Put the collet punch into the top of the tubing and tap it down firmly with a mallet; this will force the top of the tubing outward to fill the collet-block hole. Make sure that the tubing becomes completely round, then knock it out of the block.

3 The tubing should now be tapered. You will have to burr out a ledge from the inside, as described left, to be able to set the stone.

282 Making a collet using a template

You can also make your own tapered collet without using tubing. This is particularly useful if you want to set a large stone, since you can't buy tubing larger than 6mm (¼in) outside diameter. First you need to work out the template of the setting for the size of stone that you are using. Making a collet can be difficult, as you need to work out the shape required to create the right arc to produce a cone-like shape. Shown below at actual size is a template for a collet setting for a 10-mm (³⁄₈-in) stone.

Transfer this template onto metal and pierce it out, then file and sand the edges. Anneal the piece of metal, then, bend the two ends together until they meet, using round-nose pliers. Get a good seam and solder the two ends together, then pickle and wash.

Make sure the setting is dry before you place it in the right-sized collet-block indentation, then put the collet punch into the setting and tap it down with a mallet until it is round. Take the setting out of the collet block. File and sand the solder seam. The setting is ready to be soldered onto your jewellery design.

Tapered collet template

Tapered collet settings
Silver rings using the 10-mm (³⁄₈-in) collet to set a blue topaz and a lemon quartz.

283 Making a setting for an irregular stone

This is a simple way of setting an odd-shaped stone, using round wire. It works well if you want the stone to be the focal point of the piece of jewellery, because with this technique all you should see from the front of the piece are the four bobbles of silver that hold the stone in place. It works well with fairly large, odd-shaped stones. You can also use this technique for setting interesting pebbles, sea glass or other found objects. You will need round wire to make the setting, and the thickness will depend on the size of stone that you are setting: try 1– 1.5mm (18–14 gauge).

Sea-glass pendant
A piece of irregular-shaped sea glass set with a simple claw setting. All you can see from the front are the bobbles holding the glass.

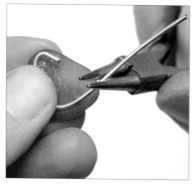

1 Decide which side of your stone you want the front to be, then, using round-nose pliers, shape a long piece of the wire to mirror the shape of the back of the stone, just in from the edge. When you are happy that it is the right shape, saw off where the wire overlaps and file the two ends at right angles.

2 Solder these two ends together, using hard solder. Pickle and wash. File the excess solder from the seam and check the shape again, making sure that it still fits the profile of the stone. Use masking tape to fix the wire loop to the back of the stone; this helps to keep it from moving while you are taking measurements.

Chunky claw setting
An emerald-cut citrine set in an unusual claw-type setting using rectangular wire.

3 Mark four points on the wire loop on the back where the claws are going to be soldered, usually two at the bottom and two near the top. Also mark where the bail will be for a pendant.

4 Cut four pieces of wire longer than you need to make the claws, then put one into a pair of reverse-action tweezers, which will hold the wire securely. Turn on the torch and put it on the workbench, then bring the wire into the flame at the hottest point. The wire will become bright red and the end of the wire will begin to melt and form a small bobble. Do this to all four wires.

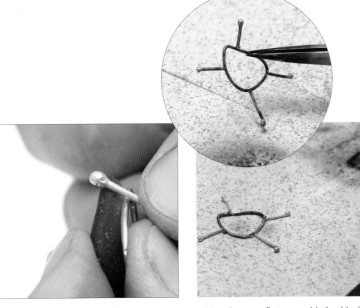

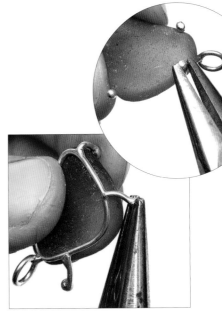

5 Sand the bobbles as smooth as you want them. Using scrap wire, measure from the mark you made on the back of the wire loop on the stone to just around the front of the stone, following its contours. Transfer this measurement to the wire with the bobble, measuring from the start of the bobble down, then make a mark on this piece of wire and saw it off at this length. Each wire claw will be a different length, so make sure you mark which is which.

6 Lay them out flat on a soldering block. Flux where they join, then put a piece of fluxed medium solder on each seam and heat the whole thing until the solder runs. Pickle and wash. File and sand any excess solder. You can then solder a jump ring on the top to make it into a simple pendant, remembering that this and any subsequent soldering should be done with a lower temperature solder – ideally extra-easy, so that you don't melt the solder on the wires.

7 Now polish the piece in a barrel polisher (not on a polishing wheel); if you don't have one, you can polish using attachments on a drill. To set the stone, put it into the wire and start to push the wires around the stone with your hands. Then use round-nose pliers to get the wires to bend in a little tighter to the stone, until it is gripped.

284 Setting found objects

It can be interesting to use unorthodox objects as a focal point in your jewellery design and there are many different ways of setting objects such as slate, fossils or ceramics. Often the specific object will dictate what sort of setting you will use; simple claws work well with objects of varying depths, or you could decide to drill and rivet the piece. Whatever option you choose, you can create interesting alternatives to traditional settings in order to create unique designs.

This shell has been set with simple silver claws to hold it in place.

An irregular-shaped piece of drusy, showing its different depths. You could set this with claws to make a feature out of its unusual dimensions.

Reticulated silver ring
*Learn how to reticulate metal using the helpful
information in tip number 222 on page 93.*

CHAPTER FIVE:

Simple jewellery design for metalwork

This chapter will give you an insight into many aspects of designing and planning for metalwork pieces, from sizing a ring and recording and harnessing inspiration to planning the details of a piece and choosing finishings and findings. There are more tips and techniques for designing with beads on pages 14–15.

Developing design ideas

It can be a challenge to know where to start with designing your own jewellery. Often the temptation is to copy a design that appeals to you. To design your own original pieces takes time and research, but it's worth the effort.

FIX IT

286 MAKING IT BETTER

Look at a piece of jewellery you own, perhaps even one that you have made and analyse its design elements. See if there is anything you would change – size or choice of colours or stones, perhaps – and draw the changes you would like to make to it.

285 Find your design approach

You do not have to be limited to one approach for realizing your design dreams. Here are productive ways to think creatively:

- **Using a process** Use a particular technique as the main element of the design and show it off to its best advantage – for instance, using the rolling mill to inlay different-coloured metals could become the main feature of a design.

Cubed ring
The 18-karat gold cubes that constitute this ring by Peter de Wit are hollow and have been scored and bent to give them their characteristic form.

- **Conveying an idea or emotion** Take an idea such as 'freedom' or 'love' and try to convey that idea through imagery or more abstract means to create a jewellery design.

- **Using an object or image as a starting point** Start off by looking at something specific, such as an Art Deco piece or shells, then work on the shapes, colours and forms that the object or image suggests to you and translate them into design ideas.

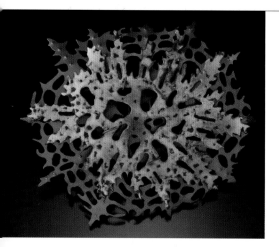

'Metaphor for Death'
Part of Anne Havel's 'Haeckel Ocean Series', this piece is inspired by the cellular structure of sea creatures as they decompose. It is made from torch-fired vitreous enamel on copper.

Freedom pendant
This piece was inspired by the idea of escape and uses the words 'sail away with me' engraved into the pendant to reinforce the message.

TRY IT

287 **KEEPING A SKETCHBOOK**
Sketchbooks are great for recording ideas. Some are destined never to be completed, but it's useful to look back and possibly rework old ideas. Use it to keep cuttings that might stimulate ideas for a piece of jewellery. Also keep test pieces of ideas, such as textures. When you are making a piece of jewellery, it's a useful idea to keep a record in your sketchbook of solders used, as well as costs and measurements. If you want to make another similar piece, this takes away much of the guesswork.

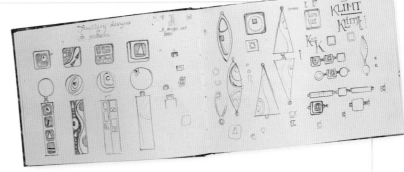

288 ## Design considerations checklist

This checklist highlights the key considerations you need to bear in mind during the design process. It makes sense to have a clear idea of how you want the finished piece to be, even if you change small details of the design along the way.

- **Shape** Do you want the piece to be uniform, geometric, symmetrical or asymmetrical? Try to ensure that the scale of elements being combined is visually pleasing.
- **Form** Do you want a piece to be seen from all angles? It can be good to make the back of a piece as interesting as the front.
- **Finishes** What kind of finishing or patterning do you want, if any? This will greatly alter the finished result and its visual appeal. Consider a matte finish, enamelling and so on.
- **Colour** Do you want the piece to be monochrome, to have natural colouration, or be intensely coloured through the use of stones, enamelling or resin?
- **Wearability** Will the piece be practical and comfortable to wear?
- **Materials** What material(s) can you use to make the piece strong, wearable and visually pleasing?
- **Budget and time** How much money and how long you have to make your piece will affect your decisions for all of the above points.
- **Skills** It's good to challenge yourself, but be realistic about the techniques you have learned and the tools and materials you have available.

Stone shape
David Fowkes' pendant design is driven by the unusual organic shape of the opal stone. The diamond was subsequently welded into place using laser technology.

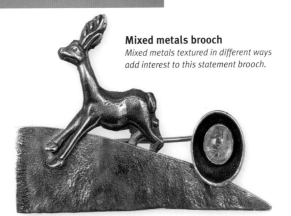

Contrasting colours
This ebony and coral pendant by Aaron Barr uses sharp graphic contrasts to get attention. The wood is hand cut with a scroll saw and hand textured with jeweller's burrs.

Mixed metals brooch
Mixed metals textured in different ways add interest to this statement brooch.

289 Turning 2-D ideas into 3-D realities

Once you have a rough sketch of the design you want to create, you need to work out the practicalities of how to achieve it – what materials to use and also the scale. Use rulers and graph paper to help you draw your design to scale, remembering to draw side and back views. If you change the dimensions of a design, this can greatly alter it visually. For instance, changing a ring band from 1.5mm (¹⁄₁₆in) to 9.5mm (³⁄₈in) will be a dramatic change. Sometimes a piece can look good when it's drawn large, but can become difficult to make at actual size.

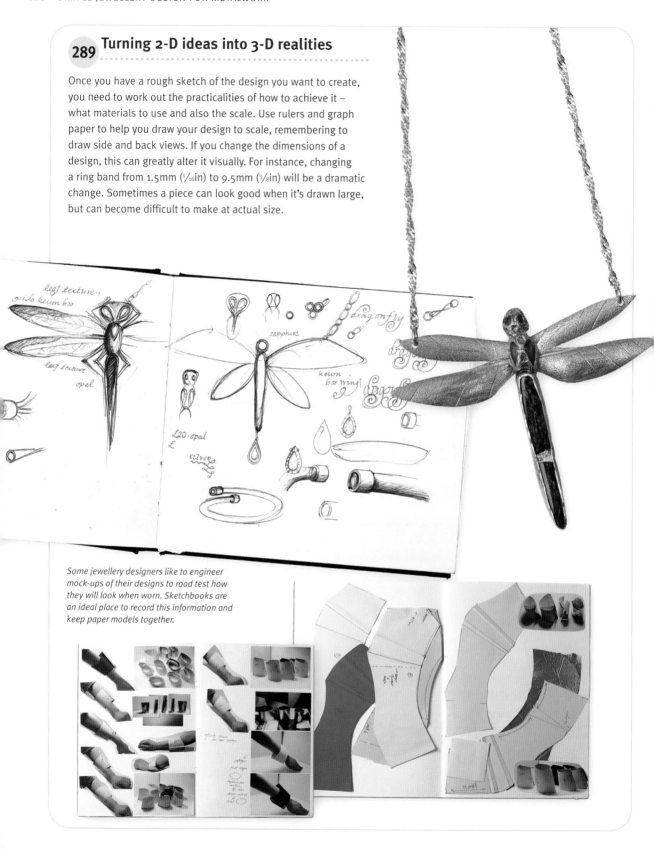

Some jewellery designers like to engineer mock-ups of their designs to road test how they will look when worn. Sketchbooks are an ideal place to record this information and keep paper models together.

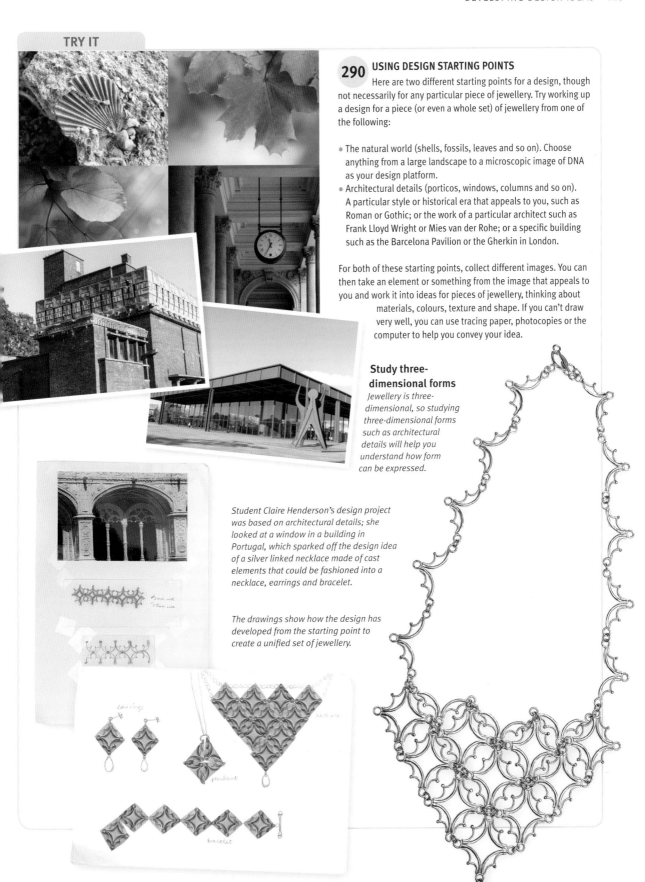

TRY IT

290 USING DESIGN STARTING POINTS

Here are two different starting points for a design, though not necessarily for any particular piece of jewellery. Try working up a design for a piece (or even a whole set) of jewellery from one of the following:

• The natural world (shells, fossils, leaves and so on). Choose anything from a large landscape to a microscopic image of DNA as your design platform.
• Architectural details (porticos, windows, columns and so on). A particular style or historical era that appeals to you, such as Roman or Gothic; or the work of a particular architect such as Frank Lloyd Wright or Mies van der Rohe; or a specific building such as the Barcelona Pavilion or the Gherkin in London.

For both of these starting points, collect different images. You can then take an element or something from the image that appeals to you and work it into ideas for pieces of jewellery, thinking about materials, colours, texture and shape. If you can't draw very well, you can use tracing paper, photocopies or the computer to help you convey your idea.

Study three-dimensional forms

Jewellery is three-dimensional, so studying three-dimensional forms such as architectural details will help you understand how form can be expressed.

Student Claire Henderson's design project was based on architectural details; she looked at a window in a building in Portugal, which sparked off the design idea of a silver linked necklace made of cast elements that could be fashioned into a necklace, earrings and bracelet.

The drawings show how the design has developed from the starting point to create a unified set of jewellery.

Designing earrings and studs

The shape and form of earrings on the ear are restricted in terms of size because of their proportion in relation to the size of the ear. Despite size restrictions, earrings come in many different forms, but they all either have to fit through a pierced hole in the ear or be attached as a cuff or clip, worn singly or in multiples.

Asymmetric earrings

These earrings by Janis Kerman are a great example of non-identical pieces that are nonetheless in harmony. Made with oxidized silver to contrast with the 18-karat yellow gold.

BEGINNERS START HERE!

291 Making stud earrings

You can buy ready-made ear pins and scrolls to solder onto a stud you have made.

1 Put the stud you have made on the soldering sheet. Flux the back of it and the end of the ear pin (the end that doesn't have the indent in it, which is where the scroll sits when in your ear).

2 Use reverse-action tweezers to hold the ear pin in place on the back of the stud. Cut a small piece of low-grade solder (easy or extra-easy) and flux it, or use a small amount of syringe solder, on the end. Heat the two pieces up evenly, until the solder runs into the seam. Pickle and wash them.

292 Mixing it up

Two earrings in a pair don't have to be identical. It can be interesting to experiment with designing asymmetrical 'pairs'.

- One stud with one drop.
- Related subjects, such as a tortoise and a hare.
- Use the same technique, but have different shapes.
- Use different materials for each earring.

293 EAR PINS COMING UNSOLDERED?

If the stud is thick enough, you can drill a small hole in it the same diameter as the ear pin, where you want the ear pin to be soldered. Buy the longest ear pins you can and use reverse-action tweezers to hold the ear pin in place in the hole. Solder as described above. This method gives a larger contact area for the metal, making the seam stronger.

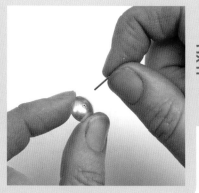

FIX IT

TRY IT

294 DESIGN EARRINGS FOR SOMEONE YOU KNOW

Because earrings are worn close to the face, they need to suit the individual wearer.

Think about their personality, face shape, hairstyle and colour preferences. If the wearer has short hair, very dangly earrings might be suitable and striking, because they will be very visible. Or perhaps the wearer is more understated and traditional, in which case a simple pair of pearl studs may be more suitable.

295 Choosing the right weight and wire

Most earrings are worn through a piercing in the ear, therefore you have to take into account the weight and wearability of the design. If they are too heavy they can pull the ear lobe and damage the skin. Also, ear wires shouldn't be thicker than 0.8mm (20 gauge), otherwise they may damage the pierced holes.

Designer Amy Holton finds sketching out her ideas a vital part of the design process. The evolution of her work from concept to reality is clear here.

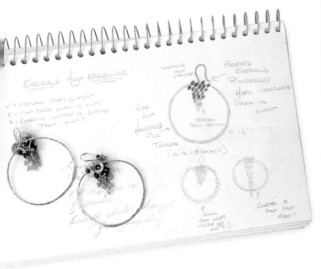

296 Earring styles

Use these traditional designs as a starting point for your own creations: make your own earring wires to create more personalized pieces. If you want to make large earrings, without the weight, use lightweight materials such as aluminium or make a hollow form, so that they look chunky while being lightweight.

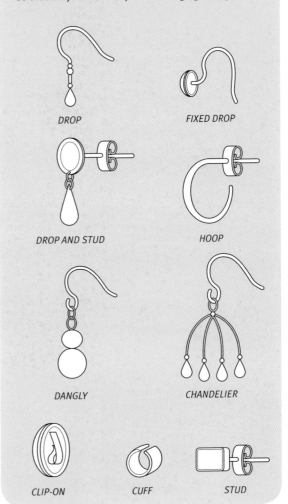

DROP — FIXED DROP

DROP AND STUD — HOOP

DANGLY — CHANDELIER

CLIP-ON — CUFF — STUD

297 Allergies

Some people are allergic to metals – particularly base metals, though sometimes also silver. The most hypoallergenic metals to use for ear wires are niobium, titanium and surgical steel, so it's worth thinking about using these materials if an allergic reaction is a possibility.

Designing rings and bangles

Rings have traditionally been given as love tokens, with the most well-known examples being engagement and wedding rings. A ring can be a very personal and sentimental piece of jewellery. Rings are small and need to be a precise fit, which can make them a challenge to design and make to scale.

Cabochon ring
This design by Emma Farquharson is an interesting take on a simple cabochon bezel setting. The fire opal is set in 18-karat gold on a silver ring shank.

298 Sizing your ring: the low-tech method

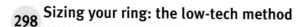

This is a simple but effective way of working out the size for your ring.

1 First decide which finger you want to make the ring for. Cut a long strip of paper a similar width to the ring band you are going to make. Wrap the strip of paper tightly around the widest part of that finger; this is usually the knuckle. Make a clear mark where it overlaps; this is the inside diameter of the ring size.

2 Now decide what thickness and profile of metal you are going to make the ring from. Transfer the mark from the paper onto the metal.

299 Design ideas for rings

There are many different design ideas you can start with. Whether you begin with a stone or a particular texture, it helps to draw up some initial ideas and then try to work out the final shape and the materials you will need.

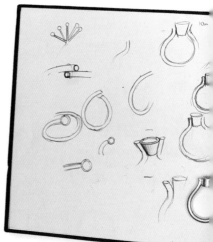

Exploring ideas
Here the jeweller auditions different ring design ideas before settling on the design that is shown in the bottom right of the page.

3 Mark on the metal the thickness of the metal you are using, plus half again – so if you were using 1.8-mm (14-gauge) metal, your paper strip would be 3mm (⅛in) wide (if you didn't add this amount, the ring would be too small). If you are texturing your ring band you must do this before you make the mark for the length of the band, because texturing stretches the metal.

4 Using a scriber and a steel rule, mark onto the metal at a right angle. Saw the ring band to length, cutting it a tiny bit bigger than required, so that you can file back to the line.

300 Different forms of rings

From plain bands to rings set with stones, rings offer the jeweller lots of design opportunities; always avoid sharp edges on the inside of a ring.

PLAIN BAND

UNSOLDERED BAND

OVERLAPPING BAND

SINGLE STONE

ETERNITY RING

STACKING RING

PUZZLE RING

SIGNET RING

TRY IT

302 SIZING THE RING ON THE MANDREL

One way to ensure that you get the ring size correct is to work the metal directly on the mandrel. Take a long piece of your chosen profile and thickness of annealed metal and bend it around the mandrel, tapping with a mallet, to create a loop. Take it off the steel mandrel and put it onto a sizing mandrel. Adjust it to the size you want, then saw through the overlapping loop to create the ring band. The two ends will need to be realigned and soldered together (see page 132).

TRY IT

303 USING AN ELLIPSE TEMPLATE

A useful tool when you are drawing your ring design is an oval template. Draw an ellipse, draw a line down from each end of this ellipse the width you want your ring band to be, then draw another ellipse at the bottom of these lines. This will give you the impression of a 3-D ring. You can use this to draw on your design features, such as stones, wire, etc.

301 Using a ring sizer

You can use a ring sizer to find your correct size. Once you have this measurement, use the chart below to find the linear measurement for it. You will still have to add on a thickness-and-a-half of the metal you are using to make the ring.

Ring size chart

US	UK	mm
3	F	44.5mm
3.5	G	45.2mm
4	H	46mm
4.5	I	47.6mm
5	J	49.2mm
5.5	K	50.8mm
6	L	52.4mm
6.5	M	53.2mm
7	N	54mm
7.5	O	55.6mm
8	P	57mm
8.5	Q	57.8mm
9	R	58.7mm
9.5	S	60.3mm
10	T	61.9mm
10.5	U	63.5mm
11	W	65mm
11.5	X	65.9mm
12	Y	66.7mm

The sizer in action.

BEGINNERS START HERE!

304 Making a foolproof ring band

This sequence shows how to make a simple ring band, which, once mastered, you can start to embellish and experiment with different design ideas.

1 Once you have cut the ring band to the right length for your ring size, you need to join it together. File the two ends of the ring band at right angles. The most important thing is to have very straight edges on the two ends to be joined – the better the fit, the better the solder seam.

2 Use two pairs of flat-nose pliers, one at each end. You can protect the ring from the pliers by wrapping the jaws in masking tape or by using plastic-covered pliers. Bend the two ends together. It doesn't matter what shape the ring is in at this point, but it is important to get the two ends touching each other as much as possible, all the way along the seam. Hold the seam up to the light to see if there are any gaps.

3 Put the ring on the soldering sheet, flux the seam and cut a medium piece of solder. Flux it and place it at the bottom of the seam, making sure that it is in contact with both sides of the seam. Light the torch and heat the whole ring evenly all the way around, ensuring that one side of the seam doesn't get hotter than the other, because the solder will jump onto the hottest side. Once the metal reaches the temperature at which the solder melts, the solder will run up the seam. Pickle and wash the ring.

4 Dry the ring thoroughly and place it on the ring mandrel. Brace the top of the mandrel against the bench and, using a mallet, hammer the ring with a downward motion while slowly turning the mandrel, so hitting all the way around the ring.

5 Look down the end of the mandrel to see if there are any gaps. Once the ring is completely round, remove it from the mandrel. Sometimes the ring can get stuck on the mandrel. If this happens, turn the mandrel upside down, put the end on the workbench and knock the ring off using a mallet.

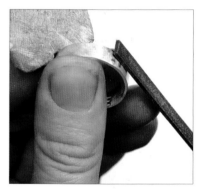

6 Check that the ring fits the correct finger. Use a flat file to file the seam, to remove any excess solder and make the seam disappear. Also file the two top edges to make the sides line up with each other. You can then use a half-round file to file the inside seam of the ring. Move down through the different grades of sandpaper to remove the scratches made by the file.

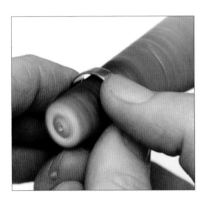

7 To polish the inside of the ring, attach a finger felt to the polishing wheel and place the ring over the end of it. Make sure you have a good hold on it while polishing.

FIX IT

305 **VISIBLE SEAM?**
When you've soldered the seam, if the solder hasn't run very well you may still be able to see it. To fill the seam, run a lower grade of solder into it, flooding it all over the area concerned, then file and sand the excess solder away. This should the make the seam invisible.

TRY IT

306 **FITTING A BEZEL TO A RING BAND**
If you want to add a stone to a ring design, you generally solder the bezel onto the ring band once it has been made into a ring. This means that you have to shape the bottom of the bezel with a half-round file to fit the curve of the ring band before you can solder it on.

Simple design
A simple ring band made from oval wire with a metal cut daisy motif soldered to the ring shank.

A bangle is just a
307 **supersized ring**

Making a bangle is just like making a large ring – all the principles of designing and making are the same. Instead of using a ring mandrel to shape it, you use a bangle mandrel, which is made of either steel or wood. You can also get oval or square mandrels, to make different-shaped bangles. To solder bangles together, you will need a hand-held butane or propane torch. Use a bangle sizer to get the correct length. Don't forget that, unlike a bracelet, a bangle is fixed in size and shape, so you need to be able to fit it over your hand; allow for this when you are sizing it.

308 **Bangle forms**

There are a few different styles and shapes of bangle. You will need a bangle mandrel to shape your metal on. An open or cuff bangle is more adjustable to size for most wearers; the hinged bangle is the most technically challenging.

ROUND

OVAL

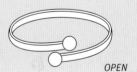

CUFF

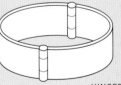

OPEN

HINGED

Lily bangle
An open-ended silver bangle, using a lily as a decorative finial.

Designing necklaces and bracelets

Necklaces can take the form of repeated units or a collection of elements that culminate in a focal point. Care must be taken that the links provide sufficient flexibility and do not bunch together when worn. In design terms, bracelets share many similarities with necklaces – the exception being bangles, which are generally rigid.

Fused bracelet
Fused silver links have been teamed with flattened ones to create an organic design in this bracelet.

309 How's it hanging?

When designing a pendant for a necklace, the aspect that often gets overlooked is how it is going to attach to the chain. When you are designing a necklace it is worth considering how to integrate the pendant into the overall design. You should also think about the influence of the material and thickness of the necklace you choose to hang the pendant on.

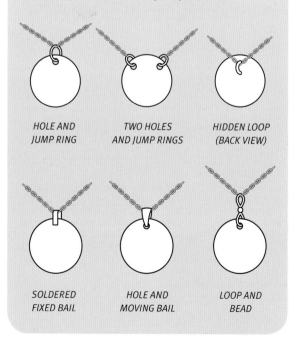

HOLE AND JUMP RING

TWO HOLES AND JUMP RINGS

HIDDEN LOOP (BACK VIEW)

SOLDERED FIXED BAIL

HOLE AND MOVING BAIL

LOOP AND BEAD

310 Design checklist

Deciding on these features is a useful starting point for your necklace or bracelet design.

Length of chain (pictured opposite)
• Collar 36–43cm (14–17in)
• Choker 41–46cm (16–18in)
• Princess 43–48cm (17–19in)
• Matinee 51–64cm (20–25in)
• Opera 66–91cm (26–36in)
• Rope 114cm (45in) +
• Lariat 114cm (45in) +

Material of chain	Choice of clasp or fitting	Design of fitting for hanging pendants or charms
• Silver	• Toggle	• Two-hole
• Brass	• Box catch	• Bail
• Copper	• S-hook	• Hidden loop
• Leather	• Bayonet	• Closed loop
• Ribbon		• Bead
• Rubber		
• Beads		

311 Standard necklace lengths

The names of the standard necklace lengths come from a tradition going back many years. Their names reflect the occasions that it was once thought appropriate to wear them. Today, they are a useful guide to the jewellery designer when planning a piece or when designing for a specific person.

Collar *(36–43cm/14–17in)* *Worn tight and high up on the neck, like a dog collar. Usually multi-strand, not recommended for people who are not comfortable wearing tight items around their neck.*

Choker *(41–46cm/16–18in) Fits very tightly around neck, lower down, just above the collarbone. Usually single-strand, suitable for formal and informal occasions.*

Princess *(43–48cm/ 17–19in) The most popular length of necklace sits high on the chest and is great with pendants.*

Matinee *(51–64cm/20– 25in) Worn down to the breastbone; suitable for casual or business wear.*

Opera *(66–91cm/26–36in) Elegant and sophisticated, but draws attention down to the chest.*

Lariat *(over 114cm/45in) Lariats are unattached at one end and so are worn knotted at the front. They can be knotted just once or multiple times and using different knots for different decorative effects.*

Rope *(over 114cm/45in) Draws attention to torso since it's quite long, but it can be shortened by double- or multi-stranding or by being knotted in front.*

312 Hidden gems

When you are designing a piece of jewellery, it's worth visualizing all the angles it can be seen from. Think beyond the front of the piece; though this is the most visible part when it is being worn, it is not the only place worthy of decoration. Think about the back, the sides and the inside. You could engrave a secret message on the back of a pendant (right top) or go beyond necklaces and bracelets and include extra stones on rings (right bottom). The main tension-set red spinel is visible from the front, but the tiny flush-set stones at the ends of the wire profile are only revealed as you move your hands. These little sparkling secrets bring a unique element to the piece.

BEGINNERS START HERE!

313 Making a linked soldered bracelet or necklace

This sequence shows how to create links and solder them together, but you can vary the shapes and profiles of your links to suit your needs. Try doubling up links and using different metals together to create your own unique design.

1 Find an object with the diameter that you want your links to be. Different sizes of dapping punches are useful for this – the tool's diameter will be the inside diameter of the link. Take your piece of wire and begin to wind it tightly, creating a coil.

2 Slide the coil off the punch, then wrap masking tape all the way around the coil of wire; this helps keep the coil from being too springy when you saw through it.

3 Put a saw blade into the top nut of the saw frame, then put the blade through the centre of the coil of wire and do the bottom nut up, trapping the coil inside the saw.

4 Saw the coil from the inside out. Take off the masking tape and you will have all the first size of links you need. With a mallet, realign the two ends of each link, making sure that the seam is tight, then solder together using hard or medium solder.

5 Make more links of a different size using thinner wire, using the same technique. If the wire is thinner than 1mm (18 gauge), you can use a pair of snips to cut the coil, but each end of the seam will then need filing straight. Don't solder these links yet.

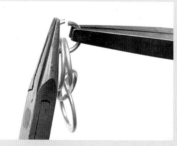

6 Using flat-nose pliers, open up the small links, put them together with the large links, and close them up tightly. Flux all the seams on the unsoldered links and put the first link into reverse-action tweezers, then put the tweezers on a block, so that the rest of the chain is hanging down. Put a small dab of easy syringe solder on the seam.

7 Light the torch and, using the flame horizontally, heat the link evenly across the seam. Don't direct the heat downwards, since this will heat up the rest of the chain. Heat until the solder flows across the seam.

8 Repeat this soldering process for the rest of the unsoldered links. Pickle the chain and wash it. (This will only work if you preflux all of the unsoldered links before you start soldering.) Decide which clasp you are going to use (see pages 137–138) and solder this onto one end.

314 How to polish a chain

Chains are not suitable for polishing on a wheel; the safest way to polish them is with a barrel polisher. Put the chain you want to polish in the barrel polisher for around one hour. If you don't have access to a barrel polisher, you could use polishing mops on a pendant drill, but you must be very careful. Polish one link at a time while holding the rest of the chain out of the way in your hands, and always wear goggles.

Using different-shaped links
This necklace by Loretta Dwane uses oblong-shaped silver links to create an unusual and unique design.

Bracelet design forms

317

Bracelets can be made from chain or from separate linked elements, or they may be multi-stranded or feature set stones. Since bracelets are worn on the wrist they are subjected to heavy wear – they get rested on, knocked and are liable to get caught around things. This means they need to be strong, secure and wearable. Charms are also very popular on bracelet designs, hanging either from a linked bracelet or from a beaded chain. These may be ready-made charms or you could make your own from sheet metal or wire.

FIX IT

315 CAN'T FIND THE BALANCE POINT?

One of the hardest things when hanging a pendant, particularly if it is asymmetrical, is finding the balance point. Before you solder a bail or drill any holes, use a pair of tweezers to lightly hold the pendant where you want the bail. You should be able to tell if it is going to hang properly. If it does not, move the tweezers slightly until you find the balance point.

TRY IT

318 TEXTURING LINKS

Planishing (hammering) gives a nice effect on thick chain links. To achieve this you need to solder the links first, then, using a flat steel hammer and a steel block, hammer the rounded links flat. You can leave them like this or put a pattern on them using different hammers (see page 90).

TRY IT

316 FIND THE NUMBER OF BRACELET LINKS

Measure your wrist size with a piece of paper. This gives you the length for your bracelet. Now work out how big you want each link to be and measure its diameter. Measure the diameter of the smaller links and add them to the length. This will give you the approximate number you need, but always make a couple more of each to allow for mistakes – and don't forget to allow for the length of the clasp.

319 Clasp design forms

There are a variety of ready-made clasps available to buy, although it can be a nice design feature to make your own for necklaces and bracelets.

S-HOOK   TRIGGER CATCH: GOLD   BAR FOR TOGGLE CLASP   BOLT RING   TRIGGER CATCH: SILVER   CIRCULAR T-BAR TOGGLE   FISH-THEMED HOOK AND EYE FASTENING

320 Making a toggle clasp

A toggle clasp can be used as a design feature on a bracelet or necklace. Made with a ring and a bar, it can be as simple or as ornate as you want. A simpler technique for a beginner is the S hook (see below).

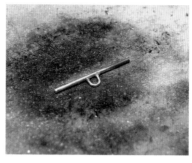

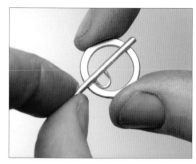

1 Begin by making a link out of wire and solder it together. Don't make the diameter of the link too big, since this will mean that the bar has to be very long. The bar length should be approximately double the inside diameter of the link. Solder a small U-shaped loop or jump ring to the centre of the bar.

2 The bar and the link can then both be joined with jump rings to the necklace or bracelet so that it can be fastened.

321 Design ideas for toggle clasps

Toggle clasps open up many design options. You could decorate the ends of the bar with balls or twisted wire, and the link doesn't have to be round – it could be square or heart-shaped. Just make sure that the bar is double the length of the widest part of the link. You can also use the toggle clasp as the main design feature of a piece and wear it at the front so that it becomes both clasp and pendant.

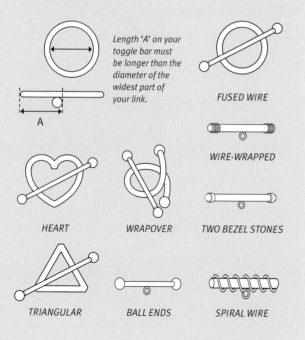

Length 'A' on your toggle bar must be longer than the diameter of the widest part of your link.

A

HEART

WRAPOVER

TRIANGULAR

BALL ENDS

FUSED WIRE

WIRE-WRAPPED

TWO BEZEL STONES

SPIRAL WIRE

BEGINNERS START HERE! 322 Making an S-hook clasp

One of the simpler kinds of clasps to make for yourself is an S-hook clasp. It is a bit like a hook and eye used on clothing, and can be made with round wire.

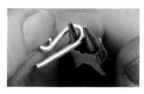

1 Choose a suitable diameter of round wire for the piece of jewellery you are making. File one end of the wire at a right angle, then, using a pair of round-nose pliers, make a round loop at the end of the wire, big enough to fit onto the last link of the chain.

2 Use a round tool, such as a mandrel or a pair of round-nose pliers, to put a larger bend in the wire in the other direction.

3 Cut the wire so that the long return of wire is past the small loop you first made and, using round-nose pliers, turn up the end of the wire and file it.

4 Put the S-hook on a steel block and, using a flat metal hammer, flatten the top part of the large loop. This toughens the wire, making the hook stronger and less bendy.

Gold and pearl brooch
This brooch by Nutre Arayavanish is made from gold-plated silver, wood sheet and freshwater pearls, using techniques such as laser cutting, engraving on wood, soldering, piercing and photo-etching.

Designing brooches and cufflinks

The visual impact of a brooch or a decorative pin is typically a simple, pleasing combination of form, colour and detail. The pin or post that is affixed to the back of the brooch needs to be considered when planning a design. Cufflinks are a popular form of masculine jewellery, having both decorative and practical functions.

324 BENT PIN?
If the pin on a brooch gets bent or is a bit bendy, you can strengthen it and straighten it: Hold the base of the pin with flat-nose pliers and, with another pair of flat-nose pliers holding the top of the pin, twist the end a few times in the same direction. This will work-harden the pin.

FIX IT

323 Design forms for brooch pins

When it comes to brooch pins there are different design styles to use, which may suit one brooch more than another. The double pin works well on large, heavy brooches because it offers more stability; a riveted pin is suitable when you can solder; and a kilt pin is fun for dangling charms or beads.

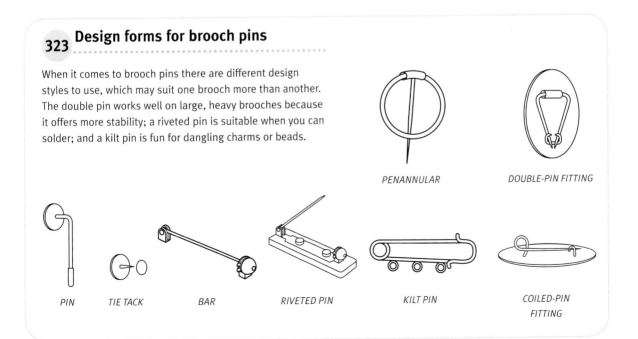

PENANNULAR

DOUBLE-PIN FITTING

PIN

TIE TACK

BAR

RIVETED PIN

KILT PIN

COILED-PIN FITTING

BEGINNERS START HERE!

325 Using a traditional brooch fitting

A traditional brooch fitting has a riveted hinge with a safety catch. You can buy these kinds of fittings or make them yourself.

Soldering the fittings

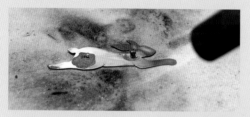

1 The hinge and the safety clasp need to be soldered onto the back of the brooch. Place your brooch on the soldering sheet with the back facing upwards. Flux the areas where the fittings will go and put the fluxed fittings in place to check that they line up. Use easy or extra-easy solder if it's your last soldering.

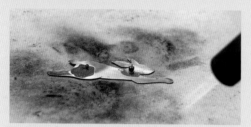

2 Use small pieces of solder, since it can run into the fittings, and keep the flame away from the fittings. Try to heat the brooch up first, since it is bigger. When the solder runs, pickle and wash the piece, check that the fittings still work, then polish your piece.

Fitting the pin

1 Use pin wire or hard wire to make the pin, or buy a ready-made one – though this limits you to the lengths that are available. Use round-nose pliers to make a small loop at one end of the wire, small enough to slot into the hinge slot.

2 Cut the other end using wire cutters. Leave it long enough that it will fit into the safety catch, then file the end to a point and sand.

Riveting the pin

Cut a short length of wire, the same diameter as the hole on the hinge and 1mm ($\frac{1}{32}$in) longer than the width of the hinge when put through the hole. File the ends at right angles. Put the edge of the hinge onto the edge of a steel block, put the wire rivet into the hole of the hinge, and, using a small riveting hammer, tap on the end of the rivet. Turn the brooch over and do the same to the other end of the wire rivet, until it is secure in the hole.

Sheet copper rabbit with a ready-made silver fitting and a hand-made pin.

TRY IT

326 A SIMPLE HAND-MADE FITTING

If you want to make a simple brooch fitting that doesn't involve riveting, the following works well on fairly large brooches.

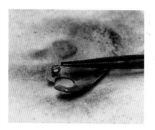

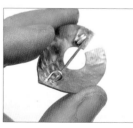

1 Use wire between 1 and 1.2mm (18 and 16 gauge), that is twice the length needed for the finished pin and make a spiral in one end with round-nose pliers. File the end and solder it to the brooch back.

2 Cut a short piece of wire from the other end of the wire and, using round-nose pliers, make a small curl. Solder it on, in line with the coil; this will become the clasp.

3 The pin will be bendy because it has been annealed through soldering, so use pliers to strengthen the wire (see page 139).

4 Bend the pin down and file and sand the end to a point. The pin should fit into the curl to secure it.

327 Double-pin fitting

This fitting for a brooch is fairly simple to make, yet stylish and very secure. You will need a small piece of round tubing and hard pin wire.

1 Cut a small piece of tubing and solder it onto the back of the brooch. This will become the hinge. Pickle and wash the brooch.

2 At the other end of the brooch, make a C-shape with a flat back from either round wire or a strip of sheet metal; this will become the clasp. Solder this with a lower grade of solder than you used for the tubing, making sure that it is in line, and sideways on to the tubing.

3 Polish the brooch. Cut a piece of 0.8–1-mm (18–20-gauge) pin wire or hard wire to more than twice the length of the measurement between the tube and the catch. Put the wire halfway through the tubing, then bend it on either side of the tubing. Bend it so that when it springs back out, it is trapped inside the C-clasp.

4 File the two ends of the wire into points and sand them.

BEGINNERS START HERE! ## 328 Soldering a cufflink fitting

Cufflinks either have a chain-type fitting or a fixed swivel fitting. In this sequence, ready-made fixed swivel fittings are used. They are probably the easiest to work with and are available in different profiles and weights. They leave you free to focus on the part of the design that will be seen.

1 File the bottom of the cufflink fitting, which sometimes has a little bump on it that will keep it from soldering properly.

2 Flux the back of the cufflink and the bottom of the fitting. Put one arm of the fitting into a pair of reverse-action tweezers and put the fitting in place on the back of the cufflink. Place a small piece of fluxed solder next to the fitting. Use the lowest-grade solder you can. Light the torch and begin heating up the cufflink base first. Then, once the solder flows, pickle and wash.

329 Cufflink forms

Here are three different forms of cufflinks. There are different designs for ready-made fittings, with different profiles of metal, but these are the most popular.

SWIVEL-ARMED CUFFLINK

DOUBLE-ENDED CUFFLINK

BAR- OR BULLET-ENDED CUFFLINK

Found objects necklace
Make use of everyday items and try incorporating buttons into your jewellery using tip number 363 on page 152.

Chapter Six

Working with non-traditional materials

This section provides an overview of some of the other materials besides traditional metals and beads that you can design and create beautiful jewellery with.

Polymer clay

Polymer clay has become well established as a jewellery-making material. It is an inexpensive medium to work in and, if you allow plenty of time, you can achieve really impressive results.

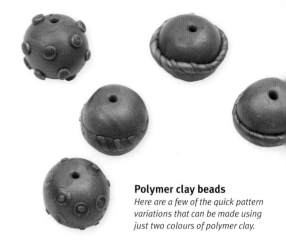

Polymer clay beads
Here are a few of the quick pattern variations that can be made using just two colours of polymer clay.

330 Go wild!

Coloured polymer clay can be mixed, layered and manipulated, then baked to create all sorts of beads and jewellery pieces. You can add powders and foils to create metallic effects. You can also incorporate wires, glass beads, natural materials – basically anything that can be heated to the same temperature as the clay. You can paint, varnish, polish and drill pieces after baking. There are several different brands, all with slightly different qualities; try them

TRY IT

332 USING A PASTA MACHINE
You can start to work with the very basic tools listed right, but you will quickly find that a pasta machine becomes an essential. You can use it to condition clay, mix colours and make smooth, even sheets of clay.
Keep a dedicated machine for conditioning clay – and don't use it for food.

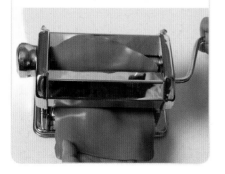

331 The essential kit

Following are the essential tools you will need to start to work with polymer clay. Many of them can be found in your kitchen – though once you use them for polymer clay, you cannot put them back there again. Polymer clay is nontoxic if handled correctly and the advised baking times are adhered to, but do use your common sense.

• **Work surface:** You will need something smooth to work on, such as a ceramic or glass tile. Kitchen chopping boards can also work; you can always add a sheet of baking parchment for a smoother surface.

• **Cutting tools:** A craft knife (1) is useful for intricate cutting, but a tissue blade (2) is essential for more advanced work (available from many polymer-clay suppliers). Remember that these are made for cutting human flesh, so they are very sharp – mark the blunt edge so you don't get confused.

• **Rollers:** For most designs you will need to flatten and smooth the clay. Plastic rollers (3) are ideal and glasses (5) and bottles (4) are another option.

• **Piercing tools:** You are likely to be making beads or designs that require holes for hanging. You can use cocktail sticks or different needles (6) to make holes in your unbaked beads. Baked polymer clay can be drilled if you prefer to make holes later.

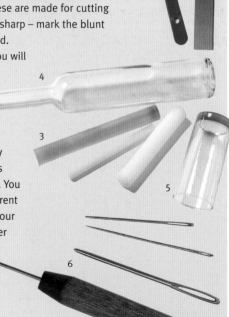

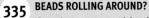

333 Get cooking

Polymer clay must be baked to harden it. To achieve this, you'll need access to the following items.

- **Oven**: A toaster oven is the most practical way to bake your clay, because you can put it in a well-ventilated space away from food preparation areas. If you do use a domestic oven, a fan oven is best. Try baking the clay in a lidded dish or using a large roasting bag – this way you can be sure that none of the chemicals from the polymer clay will remain in the oven.
- **Oven thermometer**: You will get much better results (and be safer) if you use a thermometer to check the temperature of your oven. In this way you can accurately follow the baking temperatures given on the polymer-clay packaging.
- **Baking surface**: You can bake pieces on a tile or a metal tray if you don't mind having a shiny side to your designs. To avoid this, try using baking parchment, or baking beads on a metal rod to preserve the shape all around them.

Polymer clay does smell as it bakes, and this is normal – but it should never be cooked at too high a temperature. Never use a microwave to bake polymer clay, because it will be much too hot.

FIX IT

335 BEADS ROLLING AROUND?

If you don't want to cook beads on a rod and they are rolling around on the baking parchment, try using polyester fibrefill. This can withstand the baking temperature and cushions the beads.

TRY IT

336 EXPANDING YOUR TOOLKIT

You will find that the more you work with polymer clay, the more tools you will want to add to your collection. Texturing tools might include shaped cutters, graters or extruders; you might find yourself using a garlic crusher as a tiny extruder. Old credit cards are great for indenting canes or lifting polymer clay from your work surface.

FIX IT

334 OVERWORKED HANDS?

Remember that your hands are your most important jewellery-making tool: look after them. Have some wipes and paper towel close by to use to keep your hands clean. Stop working at regular intervals and do some gentle hand and wrist exercises. You can wear latex gloves while you condition the clay; this is not essential, but it will reduce your exposure to the plasticizers in the clay.

BEGINNERS START HERE! 337 Getting the clay ready to work

It is essential that you condition polymer clay well before you start working it. You can do this very easily by hand.

1 Start by pressing a small block of the clay from the sides, then roll it between your palms or on your tabletop.

2 Fold the roll of clay in half and keep conditioning until you can fold it easily and there is no cracking or crumbling. The clay should feel malleable and soft, but not sticky.

338 Making basic beads

Here's how to get started making very simple beads. This technique is just a starting point.

1 Make a roll of conditioned clay and cut sections for your beads. You can shape them by rolling them in your palms or press in from either side with your fingers to create squares or triangles.

2 Make a hole through the centre of each bead by working a needle or cocktail stick in from either end. Try to use a drilling movement so that you don't distort the beads. Now you can bake them.

339 Making a polymer clay pendant

Polymer clay can be used to make simple, brightly coloured, bold pieces of jewellery such as pendants. You can try making a pendant with a flat piece of polymer clay decorated with another colour as elaborately or simply as you like.

1 One way to make a pendant is to put two small balls of polymer clay together as shown. Using a clear piece of acrylic or glass over the top of the balls, make circular movements until the colours mix in a pleasing way.

2 You can either make a hole at this stage, or make a small mark and drill later.

TRY IT

340 ACHIEVING GREAT SHINE

For a professional finish and to remove any finger marks, try using wet-and-dry sandpaper. Work from 800 grit down through 600 to 400, using water as you do it so there isn't any dust. You can try buffing the beads with a cloth or on a polishing wheel. There are also special polymer-clay varnishes that you can use to get a similar effect.

FIX IT

341 CLAY MUCH TOO FIRM?

If the polymer clay is very firm, start by cutting thin slices, then use your roller to work them together. Keep lifting and rolling until it is conditioned. For extreme cases you can buy a softening agent from your polymer-clay supplier. Before you give up on older clay, try warming it; you can put it in a plastic bag and submerge it in hot water. You can also try using a food processor (do not use it for food afterwards); or you can try wrapping the clay and hitting it with a mallet!

You can also condition polymer clay in a pasta machine. This is like a mechanized version of slicing and rolling. First condition a little with your hands, then work the clay through the pasta machine. Or cut the clay into thin slices, roll them together just enough to hold together on the work surface, then put them through the machine. Always start with the widest setting, fold the clay back on itself, and roll it through again. Do this a few times until the clay is conditioned.

342 **ADDING COLOUR TO PLAIN BEADS**
You can add interest to plain beads by using tiny amounts of another colour. Here are a few options for adding colour.

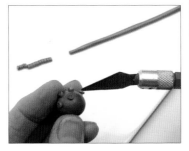

Roll a very fine strand of the second colour. You can cut tiny pieces to place around a bead to make spots. Or you can wrap a bead with the strand.

Roll fine strands of two colours and twist them together and wrap around the bead.

Cut a strand of twisted colours down the centre and open out to decorate the bead.

343 **DIFFERENT-SIZED BEADS?**
If you are worried about getting regular sizes, you can use a ruler to measure the clay sections. Reduce the length of your pieces to make smaller beads from the same roll.

FIX IT

344 **MAKING CANES**
Try making some polymer-clay canes to extend your design possibilities. Canes are made by layering colours together in different arrangements. You can then work with sections of the canes or use them to decorate other pieces.

Coiled necklace and earrings
Carol Blackburn has used tiny rolls of colour-blended polymer clay wrapped over balls of scrap clay to great effect.

Resins

In the past, resins tended to be rather toxic substances that had to be used in carefully controlled conditions. Now, however, there are many resins available that are quick, clean and easy to use. Just remember to check the manufacturer's instructions before you start.

Resin bracelet
A bracelet made from wire and polymer clay. Images were selected and then covered with UV resin.

BEGINNERS
START HERE!

345 Resin basics

UV resin is a one-part resin that will cure in direct strong sunlight (outside, not through a window) or under a UV lightbox. It is easy and fairly inexpensive to buy a UV lightbox of the kind often sold for drying nail polish quickly. UV resin is great to use for small pieces that you want to work with quickly. It can be used with baked polymer clay and papers, as well as to seal very small objects. The following steps show you how to make a start by filling a bezel.

347 BLEEDING IMAGES?

FIX IT

If you are working with pictures on absorbent paper, you will get much better results if you brush a sealant on both sides and all the edges of the paper before applying the resin.

1 Place your inclusions into your bezel. You can begin with something simple, such as a small picture, and then pour in your resin.

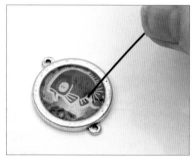

2 Make sure that the resin has filled to the edges and check that there are no bubbles. If there are, you can gently pop them with a piece of wire or a head pin.

3 Now place the piece under the UV lamp. It will need about ten minutes to cure. If you want to raise more of a dome, you can add another layer of resin and cure it again.

346 When to use a two-part resin

There are many different two-part resins available. It is a good idea to start with one that you buy from a craft supplier, since these tend to be the easiest to use. If you enjoy working with two-part resins, you can then progress to brands that are sold in larger quantities for more professional use. These kinds of resins will cure without the need for direct light, but they take longer to cure than UV resins. They are excellent for casting in moulds, using in bezels or for working directly onto photos and other objects to create lovely shiny domes. They are especially useful for larger inclusions where the UV light wouldn't penetrate far enough to cure UV resin.

TRY IT

348 LOOK, NO BEZEL!

Ready-made silver frames are used here, but you can make a frame from wire or use a large ring and put masking tape firmly behind it. Then fill it with your resin and any pieces you are including. When you remove the tape, you will have a frosted texture on the back of your piece. Put this side under the light to cure it.

349 Using two-part resin with a mould

To make everything easier for yourself, before you start to work with two-part resins gather together everything you will need – measuring cups, stirrers, a timer and something to cover the pieces while you are waiting for them to cure.

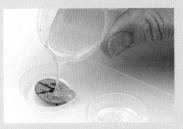  

1 Choose your mould and place your inclusions into the bottom. Now mix your resin, following the manufacturer's instructions. The resin used here needed to be mixed for two and a half minutes and then left to rest for five minutes. Pour the resin into the mould.

2 Cover the mould with a plastic box so that no dust gets in. Check after ten minutes and prick any bubbles that may have risen to the top.

3 Cover again and leave the work for 12 hours (or as long as the manufacturer's instructions specify). Now ease it out of the mould with a gentle, twisting movement.

FIX IT

350 OUT-OF-CONDITION RESINS?

If you are worried about the condition of your resins, place the bottles in a bowl of warm water before you start to work with them. This will often revive them – however, the hardeners can yellow if left unused for too long.

TRY IT

351 TAKING YOUR DESIGNS FURTHER

You can add powders and glitters to resins, as well as a multitude of different objects. Try working in layers to give the pieces depth. You can also experiment without bezels and moulds with two-part resins, or learn to make your own moulds.

353 Making flat resin pieces

Two-part resins can also be used on flat pieces without a mould. Remember that if you use paper you may have to seal it first; a drying mat is perfect for working on. Cover the pieces and leave them to cure. Once cured, you can use scissors to cut off any resin that has spilled over and file the edges. The excess will be easy to remove from the mat. Remember that you can drill the resin when it is cured.

FIX IT

352 ROUGH EDGES?

If the finished resin has rough edges, you can carefully trim them with scissors or a knife or sand them with wet-and-dry sandpaper, as for polishing polymer clay (see page 146). Try using a cushioned emery board, of the type used for filing acrylic nails.

Found objects

You can have a huge amount of fun using jewellery-making techniques with objects and materials that you find in the world around you. This can be a very different and liberating way to work.

354 Finding 'found' objects

Instead of working around a website to order metals or beads, or visiting bead and jewellery-making shops, you will find yourself searching on beaches, picking up bits of trash or choosing bottled beer because you like its top rather than its taste. Don't forget to check art supply and sewing and knitting shops – you are going to have a great time! You can choose to focus on recycled objects or concentrate on using materials that aren't always associated with jewellery making. Hopefully the ideas shown here will start you on a wonderful journey.

355 Working with bottletops

Bottletops are often like small works of art in themselves. They work wonderfully as little bezels to fill with resin.

1 Choose and fill your bottletops. (Here, stamps were used to emphasize the recycled theme. Remember to use a sealant if you have used paper in your design. Now you can fill with either one- or two-part resin and let it cure.

2 If you keep the resin quite shallow, you will be able to punch a hole in the side of the bottletop to fit findings onto. Alternatively, you can drill through the resin and the bottletop. Look at the wiring techniques on pages 32–37 to see how you would hang a pendant or earrings.

356 Horizontal wire-wrapped pendant

You may find a beautiful stone, a smooth piece of sea glass or even an interesting chunk of plastic on a beach that you love but can't think what to do with. Try wrapping it with wire to create a pendant: the following is an easy way to wrap an undrilled stone or piece of glass.

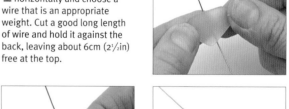

1 Hold the piece to be wrapped horizontally and choose a wire that is an appropriate weight. Cut a good long length of wire and hold it against the back, leaving about 6cm (2½in) free at the top.

2 Now wrap the wire around your piece, bringing it around the top wire each time you come to the top.

3 Repeat this about four times, then wrap the wire firmly around the top wire, perhaps finishing with a coil. Add a small bead and finish your pendant with the top of a closed loop (see page 35).

(see page 35).

TRY IT

357 BOTTLETOP NECKLACE

This does require a lot of bottletops, but you can always choose to have more beads and fewer bottletops. Use a punch or drill to make holes in the centre of the bottletops. Thread them onto a leather or cotton cord, with small beads as spacers.

358 Vertical wire-wrapped pendant

It is relatively difficult to wrap an object without a hole that you want to hang vertically. This technique takes practice, but is very rewarding once you can do it. The key to success is getting everything ready in advance ... and masking tape!

1 Cut some fine strips of tape and place them where you can reach them easily. Cut two lengths of the main wire you will be using, then wrap it in three places with short lengths of the same wire or a finer one.

2 Slightly open the main wires between the wraps, press your stone or glass against the middle wrap, and secure it with a piece of masking tape.

3 Now rearrange the wraps and tape them against the sides of the stone. Open the main wires and bring them up to the top, slightly enclosing the stone. Use your pliers to turn two of the wires from one side so that they face upwards, above the stone.

4 Wrap the other two wires together around these as close as you can to the stone, without disturbing the position of the wires too much. You can either cut these off above the wraps or leave the ends to make coil decorations.

5 Put a bead onto the other wires and finish them, working both wires at the same time, making the top half of a closed loop (see page 35). These ends can either be cut off or left to be coiled.

6 The moment of truth: remove the tape, bending the wire to either side of your stone as you do so. It should be secure, but it may be useful to 'angle' the wires to tighten them – (see Wire Too Loose, above).

TRY IT

359 EXTRA DECORATION
You can leave the ends on the side wrapping wires and coil them if you want a really decorative piece.

360 WIRE TOO LOOSE?
FIX IT

If you feel the wire isn't wrapped tightly enough, which is very likely, take a pair of chain-nose pliers and press them onto the wire in different places to gently but firmly 'angle' the wire against the stone or glass, making it tighter and more secure.

TRY IT

361 DOUBLE-DECKER
Try experimenting with using two beach finds together, by wiring one above the other, or wiring the two alongside each other.

TRY IT

362 DRILLING SEA GLASS
You can drill sea glass, but you will need diamond drill bits, and you'll have to set the drill to a very high speed. Place the glass on a piece of wood and place them both in a tub of water. Carefully hold the sides of the glass while you drill halfway through from one side, then turn the glass over and drill from the other side. Remember that you are working with electricity and water – a circuit breaker is a very good idea.

363 Incorporating buttons

Many people can remember the childhood thrill of rummaging through a button box. It is great fun to do this even when you are grown up, to find unusual buttons and think of what you could make with them. You can use the wiring techniques on pages 32–37 to make button earrings and necklaces. Try threading them, too – but be aware that buttons behave rather differently from beads.

TRY IT

364 BUTTON CUFFLINKS
Try making a quick pair of button cufflinks, using wiring techniques.

365 Button and bolt pendant

This is a great way to practise cold connection techniques. This design uses a sturdy button, polymer clay, eye pins and small brass bolts.

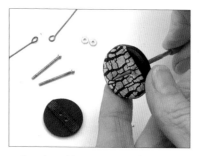

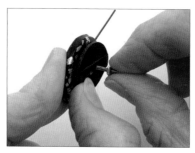

1 Start by making the polymer-clay backing piece. Condition the clay, then roll it with a sheet of foil, cut it out and bake it. Make two holes in it to correspond with the buttonholes. When it is cooked, use a file to check that the bolts will go through.

2 Now bring one of the bolts through from the back, adding an eye pin behind the polymer clay.

3 Screw the 'nut' onto the bolt. The advantage of using these little nuts and bolts is that your work is held in place at this stage. Thread on the other bolt and eye pin.

4 Clip off the ends of the bolts, leaving about 1.5mm ($\frac{1}{16}$in). Wear safety glasses as you cut.

5 Now hammer the top of the bolt in a circular movement so that it gently widens and becomes flush. Repeat for the other bolt. You can use the eye pins to create loops to hang your pendant.

367 **Crayon brooch**

Once you start to think about found items, it is very difficult not to get overexcited by the ideas that pop into your head. You will probably have lots of old pencils and crayons lying around the house, so how about trying a quick brooch? You will need a long brooch back and some wire. Here, large pencils were used for demonstration purposes, but you could use tiny crayons or pencils.

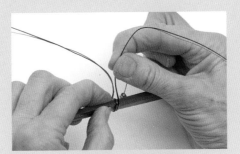

1 This example is double wrapped with two long lengths of wire. Place the pencils against the brooch back and start to wrap from in the middle.

2 Wrap as neatly as you can until you have covered the brooch back; this will keep everything secure.

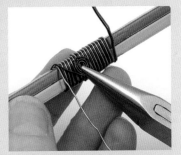

3 You can finish the wires off at the front with small coils.

TRY IT

366 UPCYCLED STATIONERY

This may be the simplest jewellery idea ever, but it gives an example of how to use everyday items to make a piece of jewellery: paperclips, with a couple of jump rings and some ribbon or cord added. It won't become a family heirloom, but it could work as an ephemeral piece.

Upcycled plastic pin
Gulnur Ozdaglar uses layers of melted PET bottles to make her beautiful pieces. She gently melts and shapes the bottles with a candle flame to avoid releasing any harmful chemicals.

TRY IT

368 MAXIMUM DRAMA

Try using the different wiring and threading skills you have learned to make a dramatic necklace from an array of many different found objects.

369 WRAPS NOT SECURE ENOUGH?

If you are finding it difficult to secure your crayon brooch with wrapping alone, there is no harm in using some glue as well.

FIX IT

Plastics

There are many different types of plastics to explore, from shrink plastic and recycled bags or bottles to the possibilities of acrylic sheets and rods. Plastic is a fantastic medium that enables you to create bold, colourful jewellery that is inexpensive to make and light to wear.

Plastic dome ring
This piece by Lesley Strickland demonstrates how plastics can be shaped and combined with metal.

370 Plastic working essentials

You can use many of the tools that you have acquired for working with metal – jewellery saws, drills and files. You can sand and polish pieces with sandpaper and polishing mops. To form plastic sheets, you will need access to a heat source (an oven). As when working with polymer clay, be very careful not to overheat the materials and create toxic fumes. Check the manufacturer's instructions and use an oven thermometer. Plastics aren't as suitable for the kitchen table as polymer clay, but if you are well organized and take safety precautions, you will be fine.

TRY IT

372 MIXING MATERIALS
You can combine plastics with other materials, including precious metals. Have a look at the brass and acrylic riveted jewellery on page 85 for inspiration.

371 Break it down

Whatever design you decide on, you're probably going to want to work with pieces cut to size. The first way to cut straight lines is by scoring and breaking.

TRY IT

1 Place a sturdy ruler where you need to cut. Run a strong, sharp knife along the edge of the ruler. Do this several times until you have scored through a quarter of the depth of the plastic.

2 With the scored line slightly overhanging the edge of the workbench, put a heavy metal block or ruler on the plastic, along the line.

3 Put one hand on top of the weight or ruler and use your other hand to press against the plastic to snap it. It should break cleanly. File the straight edges using a large flat file.

373 SCAVENGING
You can try getting off-cuts of plastic sheeting from sign makers – just ask!

374 PLASTIC NOT SNAPPING?

If you are having trouble getting the plastic to snap, try scoring again or use a heavier weight under the hand that is pressing down.

An alternative method of making a straight line is scoring and sawing.

1 Score guidelines onto the plastic, using a scriber or other sharp-pointed tool. Practise making a right angle by using a straight edge to score in two directions; this will start moving you towards making a piece of jewellery.

2 Place the plastic against the bench pin and put your saw against the scored line. Keep your saw upright and work with a gentle up-and-down movement.

3 To make the right angle, move the blade up and down a few extra times at the corner. Then turn the plastic so that the saw can continue along the other line.

375 Making a heated bangle

Try using acrylic sheet to make this simple bangle. Cut your shape, file the edges and polish the acrylic. You could make patterns within the piece before you shape it.

1 The heating can be done in a kiln or a domestic oven. Heat the oven to 170°C (340°F). Put the bracelet on a wire rack and put it in the oven for two to three minutes.

2 Use heat-protective gloves to get the acrylic out of the oven when it is soft and flexible.

3 Take a bracelet mandrel or something heat resistant with a similar shape and smooth the acrylic around it. Hold it in position; it will start to harden after about one minute.

4 When it is set and you are happy with the shape, run the bracelet under cold water to finish it.

376 WRONG TEMPERATURE?

It is very important that your oven temperature is accurate when you work with acrylic. The acrylic will bubble and be unsafe if overheated, so use an oven thermometer to be sure.

TRY IT

377 USING ACRYLIC ROD

You can make a bracelet from an acrylic rod using the technique for making a heated bangle. It will take longer to heat than the sheet acrylic, but will cool down faster, so do your shaping quickly. You can join the ends by holding them together for 30 seconds.

TRY IT

378 CURVES AND PATTERNS

Try sawing along curved lines or creating patterns within your plastic sheet.

1 First score the lines for the pattern, then drill a hole that is large enough for your saw blade, 1mm ($\frac{1}{32}$in) inside the pattern.

2 Undo your saw blade and thread it through the drilled hole with the design facing upwards. Secure the blade again.

3 Now use the bench pin for support and saw along the scored line of your design. File the curved edges with half-round files.

Index

Credits

Quarto would like to thank the following artists for kindly supplying images of their work for inclusion in this book:

Austin, Sarah, Beadsisters, www.beadsisters.co.uk, p.45t
Allene, Krueger, www.feralspassage.etsy.com, p.50tr
Gibbings, Paul, Shutterstock.com, p.54t
Dwane, Loretta, p.58, 137
Bally, Boris, www.borisbally.com. Photo: J.W. Johnson, pp.59cr, 105t
Sarah Karst Sweet Harriet Design Co. www.sweetharriet.ca, p.6tl
© 2013 Glover & Smith Designs, www.gloverandsmith.co.uk, p.61tr
William, Vanessa, www.wix.com/vrwjewellery/vrw. Photo: Craig Arnold, p.61br
McDade Jewellery, Anna, www.annamcdade.co.uk, p.74t
Cracknell Jewellery, Annie, www.anniecracknell.com, p.76tr
Peters, Felicity, www.felicitypeters.com. Photo: Victor France, p.111br
Baxter Moerman Jewellery, www.baxtermoerman.com. Photo: Hap Sakwa, p.113tr
De Wit, Peter, www.sandstrom-dewit.com. Photo: Jonas Sällberg, p.124c
Havel, Anne, www.annehavel.com, p.124bl
Fowkes Jewellery, David, www.dfjewellery.co.uk, p.125tcr
Barr, Aaron, www.aaronbarr.com, p.125bcr
Hoover, Megan R., Shutterstock.com, p.127tl
LilKar, Shutterstock.com, p.127tr
Konstanttin, Shutterstock.com, p.127btr
Fuxa, Filip, Shutterstock.com, p.127btl
MaxyM, Shutterstock.com, p.127cr
Alicar, Shutterstock.com, p.127cr
Kerman, Janis, www.janiskermandesign.com, p.128t
Cain, Susan Law, Shutterstock.com, p.129t
Holton, Amy, www.amyholtondesigns.com, p.129b
Farquharson, Emma, Emma Q Jewellery, www.emmaq.com, p.130t
Arayavanish, Nutre, Nutre Jeweller, www.NutreJeweller.com, p.139t
Blackburn, Carol, www.carolblackburn.co.uk, p.147b
Ozdaglar, Gulnur, www.gulnurozdaglar.com, p.153bl
Strickland, Lesley, www.lesley-strickland.co.uk, p.154t

All other jewellery pieces are by the authors Xuella Arnold and Sara Withers.

Thanks to Loretta Dwane for allowing us the use of her jewellery studio during the making of this book.

All other photographs and illustrations are the copyright of Quarto Publishing plc. While every effort has been made to credit contributors, Quarto would like to apologize should there have been any omissions or errors – and would be pleased to make the appropriate correction for future editions of the book.

The author and publisher can accept no liability for the use or misuse of any materials mentioned in this book. Always read product labels and take all necessary precautions.